BUILD YOUR MUSIC CAREER

FROM SCRATCH

A Step-By-Step Guide to Becoming A
Successful Artist

BY: ANDRAE ALEXANDER

Published By:
Protective Publishing Company

Printed in the United States of America

First Printing, 2014

ISBN 978-0-9904754-1-5

For more information go to:
andraealexander.com

TABLE OF CONTENTS

Introduction...1

Book One (Seeing Into Your Future)

Dream Fulfilled..9

The Window Shopper...12

Action Jackson..16

Book Two (The Book Of Questions)

Introduction...22

Should I Do Music For a Living?.........................24

How Do I Get Vocal Training?............................29

How Do I Get Confident With Performing?.....31

How Do I Get Photos and Videos Done?..........36

What is Outsourcing?..39

How Do I Fund a Project?....................................42

How Can I Get a Band Together?......................48

What is a Producer? 52

How Do I Find Music Professionals? 54

How Do I Find a Producer in a Small Town?....57

I Found a Producer, Now What?.......................61

As a Producer, How Can I Grow?......................65

What is Mixing and Mastering, Do I Need It?..69

How Do I Get My Songs Mixed?.......................72

What is a Manager, When Do I Need One?.....74

What is Publishing?...78

What Are Royalties and How Do I Get Them? 81

How Do I Sell Myself As An Artist?...................87

How Do I Network?...90

I Finished My CD, What's Next?.........................99

Book Three (Getting Your Message To The Masses)

Introduction...106

Create Your Roadmap...107

Make a Press Kit...110

Get Gigs...116

Charge to Perform...120

Use Tools Online to Gain Exposure...............126

Get Discovered...or Not!...............................130

Send Music to Record Executives...or Not!....134

Get Your Music On the Radio..........................136

Market Successfully...141

Make A Tour...149

Make Contracts..152

Conclusion..155

Resource Section

Resource Checklist..158

Road Map...160

Address book...162

Invoice...164

Press Release Check list....................................166

ABC Time Management.....................................168

Gig gear logistics...170

Technical Rider..173

INTRODUCTION

My creative heart breaks each time I hear extremely talented people say that they gave it their all, and nothing happened for them. This is a sad reality for many people, because "making it" as a music artist is most often difficult to achieve. Most artists take the time to learn how to make good music, but never learn how to successfully profit from their music. Therefore, artists generally live what might be considered a double life; one where they have to take traditional jobs to make ends meet, and the other where they pursue their dreams, when time permits.

When I hear a creative person tell me of their mishaps in life, I generally ask them the following question: "What do you want to do?" Even though the answers may vary depending on the field of art, being a musician myself, I decided to focus solely on musicians. Typically what I hear is, "I want to be a musician, and make money doing it."

This is actually a very easy thing to achieve. All you have to do is walk down the street in every major city in the world and see plenty of homeless people performing, doing just that, "making money" playing music. Knowing that most of us enjoy sleeping in our own beds at night, I assume that this is not what they mean. Basically, the answer they meant is that they want to be able to at least "make a living" doing music.

In my opinion, the biggest thing that keeps an independent artist from succeeding is not the lack of effort, but rather the lack of *focused* effort, and a clear vision of what the artist wants in his or her career. It's just like getting in your car wanting to drive "somewhere" and never getting there because you don't know where "there" might be. This is why I decided to write this book -- to help you figure out where you are going.

It is my hope that you not only read this book, but also take the time to use the advice as well as answer the questions. This will help you define what you want to achieve in your career as an artist and give you a clear cut road map on the steps to take for getting there. I also give suggestions on how to get past the excuse of not having enough money. Most people have this idea that "true" artists are those poor malnourished individuals barely surviving these tough economic times - well, any times for that matter. Even though certain artists pride themselves on living in the "starving artist" paradigm, you can choose to be true to your artistry and make a living at the same time.

The fact of the matter is that it is alright to make money and have the career you want. More artists are successful than you would believe. If you follow the exercises outlined in this book, you will have all the information

INTRODUCTION

you need to take steps in the direction of musical success. It is important to define what success is for you, however. This will allow you to know how close you are to achieving your goal.

According to *Webster's Dictionary*, "success" is defined as; "Favorable or desired outcome; the attainment of wealth, favor or eminence." Many people focus on the second part of the definition as opposed to the first part, "favorable or desired outcome." Success is nothing more than being able to set a goal and to achieve it. Yet, many artists believe that in order to be counted as being *successful* you need to be someone like Bono or Jay Z.

Even though these artists are prime examples of being incredibly successful, their success might not be yours. Hopefully, after reading this book, you will be able to achieve success based on your current situation and abilities. Either way, if you were to ask Bono or Jay Z whether or not it was easy for them to become successful, they'll most likely say "not," and probably with an exclamation point (Not!).

This book is actually three books in one. The first book will help you to figure out exactly what it is that you want to achieve in your musical career, and then show you how to clearly define what success is for you. The "road map" that you complete in this section will be the foundation for the steps you take the rest of the book.

INTRODUCTION

The second book is designed to prepare you, mentally, for the journey that you will take in your career. Some of the topics covered are outsourcing, getting vocal lessons, obtaining photos inexpensively, the basics of publishing, and royalties. I also cover the importance of networking in this section: you will learn that there is always a person/people to deal with in this industry.

In the third book, I show you how to take your career from being a vision in your head to being a reality everyone else can also see. I show you how to create a press kit and get gigs, as well as how to submit your music to radio stations. Marketing is also a topic in this portion of the book. I also added a resource section at the back of the book that will complement the third part of the book. Your job in this book is simple: do the exercises as they are presented. If you follow my instructions, you can go from having no music to having music recorded and on iTunes, a website completed, and performances booked. Some people have had success by reading the book one complete time through, and then going back to do the work. Whatever the process you choose, please do the work.

As the music industry continues to evolve and technology becomes more inexpensive, you will still be able to apply these universal principles in the era to come, ultimately "making it" as a musician. Being a musician is not the easiest feat on the planet, but if you

INTRODUCTION

know deep down inside that you are meant to perform in front of people for the rest of your life, this book is for you. It doesn't matter if you want to be a singer, songwriter, producer, or a stage musician, all of the information that I am sharing with you will definitely help you on your way up the staircase to musical success.

Andrae Alexander

INTRODUCTION

"Once you know your worth, everyone else will too."

~.Andrae Alexander

BOOK ONE

SEEING INTO YOUR FUTURE

I have created several small assignments that require you to do a little research. These easy assignments are designed to give you a fundamental understanding of what it is you want in your career and what is needed to achieve success. Once you clearly define your goals, my hope is that your confidence will grow as you see your dreams become easier to attain

DREAM FULFILLED

Materials:
- Pen
- Paper
- Some peace and quiet

The following exercise is aimed at creating a vision. If you don't have vision for your career in music, you will never know if you actually achieved your goal or not. This exercise is meant to allow your mind to roam free of limitations and negativity. In fact, this exercise takes place in a "perfect world," where you have all the resources and time to achieve anything you want. The idea is to be very specific about what you want, and not write down ambiguous things like, "I want to be a singer or music producer".

You need to envision your career as if you have achieved your goals already, almost as if you are looking back on your life. Include things like the awards you want to win, places you want to perform, and the amount of money you want to make. Also include names of people you would want to work with, and places where you want to tour. The point of this exercise is to have fun and to explore the widest regions of your imagination.

For now, just to get started, write for at least thirty minutes before moving on to the next exercise. I specify "at least thirty minutes" because you should get into the habit of devoting time to obtaining clarity for your career and goals. The more details you can add, the better. Strap on your thinking cap and get to work. I'll be here when you get back.

DREAM FULFILLED
– CONTINUED...

Hopefully, by now you have finished putting at least the first draft of your "wants" on paper. Don't think that this exercise stops at this point, you can come back and add more things as we go along. In fact, I advise you to obtain a white board, flip chart, or big sheets of paper with your goals written on them and hang them where you will see them often.

By now, you should have a decently clear picture of what success looks like to you. Even though you might think this is a small step to take, knowing what the end of your career looks like makes it easier for you to make informed decisions. Now that we know "where" you want to go, let's start figuring out what you can do to get there.

Going from one place to another requires action and a vehicle. The word "vehicle" in this context has nothing to do with the car that you drive. The vehicle I'm talking about is your talent, or multiple talents, for those so fortunate. It is the thing that will carry you to your goals. In the next exercise, we will see what "vehicles" you can use to get you moving towards your dreams quicker.

ANDRAE ALEXANDER

The Window Shopper

Materials:
- Pen
- Paper
- Highlighter
- The Internet

In this next exercise, we will be taking a closer look at the people that inspire you, that is, the people that you consider successful artists. It is always a good idea to have "role models" or "teachers" to help you to stay on track. Pick five people that you deem as "extremely successful," and write their names on a piece of paper.

After you have written down their names, "*Google*"™ them, and see what talent they used from the beginning of their career up until now. If the "teacher" you choose is no longer alive, simply see what talent they used throughout their entire artistic career. Write a small bio on each of them that clearly explains how they started their careers, and what steps they took throughout their journey to success.

Once these bios have been written, highlight the things that you feel you already have the skills to do.

I'll use Quincy Jones as an example. The *Wikipedia*™ site states that Mr. Jones used his trumpet playing skills to play small gigs and weddings. He then landed a gig playing for

Lionel Hampton; that gig led him to arranging. He then started arranging for other bands and singers. Later, he started his own band, and did more arranging and recording. Subsequently, he started composing and arranging music for film. While working on the film, "The Wiz" he met Michael Jackson. This resulted in Mr. Jones producing the largest selling album of all time.

Do you notice the progression? He first started out with something that came natural to him, something he knew, and then he learned new skills as he went along. Nobody is born ready; the process of becoming successful requires you to evolve with every situation, to acquire new skills and to push your own boundaries. Each step Mr. Jones took gave him the knowledge and experience to be prepared for his next project. Obviously, there is no time limit to this particular exercise.

"Have fun… if it's not fun, you're doing something wrong!"

~Andrae Alexander

THE WINDOW SHOPPER
– CONTINUED...

Now that you have done some research on people you admire, I hope you can see the similarities in what they did and what you can do to move your music career in the direction of success. People tend to focus on the end result of success as opposed to the journey to get to success. A majority of famous artists had their start from lowly means, unknown and without a dime in their pockets. The thing that made them stand out among the millions of others with the same goals is the fact that they stayed focused and kept going when others quit.

You should now have a clear picture of what you want to achieve and what "vehicles" are available to get you to your destination. So, it's time to figure out how to prepare yourself when opportunity comes knocking on your door. In the words of the famous racecar driver, Bobby Unser; "Success is where opportunity and preparation meet!"

If your dream is to be a singer that makes a good living performing for large audiences, you probably should sing at other venues than your shower. You will need to build a large repertoire of songs that you can sing, as well as have professional recordings of you singing (covers and originals). Even though you may have a great personality and a killer smile, action is required to progress.

The next exercise is designed to give you even more clarity by discussing what job titles your "mentors" held or currently hold. Discovering this will give you even more clarity. Knowing what skills you may need to develop will prepare you for the opportunities that will eventually lead to your musical success.

ACTION JACKSON –TO DO LIST

Materials:

- Pen
- Paper
- Highlighter
- The Internet

The following exercise is comprised of four parts.

In the first part of this exercise, you will need to hop back on the internet saddle, and yet again do research on the successful people listed in the previous exercise. This time around, you'll focus on what *titles* are connected to these artists and write the particular title beside the artists names.

For instance, if you were to search Sean Combs on *Wikipedia*,™ it states the following: record producer, rapper, actor, singer, men's fashion designer, recording executive, performer and TV producer, to name a few.

Part two is simple, once you have finished your research on all of your "teachers," it's time to learn the job description for each title. Write a description of each of the job titles, and the responsibilities and skills needed to hold the position.

Step three of this exercise will require you to research how many **products** you can buy from your "mentors," or how many ways you can find that they are making money from the public. This could include CDs, books, perfumes, fashions, TV shows, movies, and pretty much anything you can purchase to put money into their pockets. This will give you a clearer understanding of how these artists took their name and created a business out of it. In essence, they created alternative sources of income in order to fund their creative endeavors.

The fourth and final step brings all of your research to you as an artist. Write down all of the titles, and highlight the products that you would love to be able to create and sell. This step will give you an outline of how you can make money using talents that you have or are willing to develop.

This specific exercise is designed to give you a clearer understanding of what you want to accomplish professionally. The world is a lot bigger than you may perceive. If you know how to give people the opportunity to give you money, you'll discover that your art can be more profitable than you could ever imagine.

Take as much time as you need on this exercise, the book will be here when you are done...likely. ☺

ACTION JACKSON – TO DO LIST
– CONTINUED...

I hope you enjoyed the last exercise. One thing you have to keep in mind is that your goals and objectives will change the more you learn. No one has the ability to know every detail of what will happen in the future, therefore, you must be flexible with your plans. You may start out on the journey of a music producer, and realize that you hate going to the recording studio. Be open to learning, and don't be afraid to be stretched beyond your comfort zone. Being comfortable for too long is a sign of a stagnant career.

Congratulations on getting through book one! By now, you should be clearer about what you want to achieve in your career. Book two is designed to take you from imagination to realization. The goal of this next book is connection. Networking is a major theme. You will learn how to get what you need, while helping others get what they need in return.

It doesn't matter if you are the most talented person in the universe, if no one knows you. The music industry operates on the principle of interdependency. Interdependency is simple, you need something I have, and I need something you have. Reciprocity is a key to music success.

There are very few musicians that do everything on their own. In fact, everybody relies on someone to make it happen. For example, a musician may rely on a producer to help him through the recording process; the producer then needs the audio engineer to capture the performance, and mix it to have proof of his abilities as a producer; the audio engineer then needs the musicians to play well, and the producer to produce well, so that he can have a great song mixed. They all need a great final product to get more work.

If you want to achieve success within the music industry, you will need to become an expert in relating to other people. There is also something else, a key that most artists miss, and that is "timing." If you have all of the connections, but your talent is underdeveloped, your networking efforts will not lead to your success. "Timing" means you must be prepared. Don't try to book a gig without having your press kit finished; don't try to talk to a manager before having music recorded and a few gigs under your belt.

If you are just starting off, it is essential that you become an expert in networking and timing. You need to have all materials ready, be able to back up all of your claims, and you must be consistent. You need to be able to see your own value before anyone else can. You learn your value by the victories you obtain in the recording studio and at performing gigs.

These victories can be as simple as learning good microphone technique, or as huge as consistently receiving standing ovations for a song that was difficult to sing live. Your victories will only be known to you, and may not show themselves as victories until years later when you are helping new artists get started.

However, enough of this, I'll see you in book two.

BOOK TWO

THE BOOK OF QUESTIONS

By now, you should have a clearer idea of what you want to achieve within the music industry, and also have at least a vague idea of how to achieve it. You should have studied your "mentors" and learned how they have achieved success. Hopefully, studying successful people has you thinking about your own success, and the monumental effort it will take to get you there.

Like the old saying goes, "Rome wasn't built in one day," your music career will follow a similar progression. Even though you might have a general idea of what you want to achieve, there are still plenty of things you have to know and obtain to make it happen. There are people that you have yet to meet that will help you along the way. In order to meet them, you have to get out and be social. Thanks to the internet, gaining access to resources and people has been greatly simplified.

If you have a question about something, need to know how to do something, or who holds what position at a record label, a simple internet search on *google.com* (or other search engines) will most likely get you close to your answer. Also, thanks to advances in modern technology, we all have access to equipment that, twenty years ago, would have cost the price of an entire house, yet, now can be acquired for the price of a good pair of shoes.

Book two is designed to teach you what people can help you in your career, and where to find them. This is also where you learn the basics of music publishing and networking. The information you receive will give you a vocabulary to use in your music business, as well as give you tips to record your music inexpensively.

Just so you know, to practice the concepts in this book, you will most likely need to leave the comfort of your home. One of the things I discuss is networking. Even though it is possible for you to be a "stay-at-home" musician and still make a significant amount of money, for many of us, we want to be on stage as well as on the road. Either way, you will need to network to meet the right people.

"You can't just be good at what you do, people have to actually like you."

~.Andrae Alexander

SHOULD I DO MUSIC FOR A LIVING?

From my personal experience, there are seasons for everything. I have done quite a few jobs as a musician that have made me the person I am today. I've been an active duty military musician playing for royalty, and a musician in a theater company. I've played for elementary schools, been an engineer for a record label, and been a vocal coach. I've also been hired as a music director, composer, and transcriber, to name, in reality, just a few. Until I tried all of these positions, I assumed I would love them all.

I was so excited to get my first job transcribing music for a large ensemble. After the first *hour*, I realized I hated transcribing. I was extremely bored with sitting, and listening over and over, to music to get every note correct. On top of having to proofread every note, I also had to make sure all of the note ranges and key signatures were correct for every instrument, and then make sure the chart was easy to read. Although I appreciate a well-written chart, I have no interest in being the one to create that chart.

This led me to a very important discovery. Just because you have the know-how and skill, does not mean you were meant to do a certain job. For me, the journey to figure out where should be my place in the entertainment industry started with taking every gig I was offered, and figuring out which ones made me feel the most fulfilled.

"Just because you have the know-how and skill, does not mean you were meant to do a certain job".

~Andrae Alexander

I learned that my fulfillment and happiness with my work were a barometer for determining when to move on. There were jobs that I performed that brought me joy, initially, that you couldn't pay me to do today. I learned to look at every job, and set a goal. For example, I've worked for artists that were not nice people, but they had notoriety, and working with them looked good on my resume'. I just didn't work for them for an extended period of time.

I would set a goal of doing at least one gig with them to get video footage or photos, and move on to the next gig. Once I realized that all I needed was the payment from the gig, the experience of working with different artists, and their names on my resume', I was freed from stress. Your job is to do your best on every gig, no matter the pay; if you said "yes" to the gig, treat it like you're making a million dollars.

Having said that, when you start dreading going to a place, it's time to move on. I realized that what I bring to the table, as a talented and professional musician, was just as important as everyone else's job, including the headliner performer. Once you know your worth, everyone else will too.

Knowing "what to do" in life requires you to know where you want to end up. If in twenty years you see yourself as an artist that is known for helping animals, that means you can't take a gig for the clothing designer that makes the best seal skin shoes. What you do right now, and in the fledgling portion of your career, should reflect where you are ultimately going.

If you want to be the best drummer in the world but don't want to practice, maybe you should pick another goal. If you want to be a super star, but don't want to go to the gym to work out, never want to go to the studio to record, can't take criticism, and you hate people, you may want to look at another goal.

If you love what you're doing, keep doing it. If you hate what you're doing, do something else. Don't be the person that never "lives" out of the fear of making a mistake. If you try something and fail, you are one step closer to your goal.

Of course, there are moments when your career doesn't look the way you want, and the money may not be coming in as fast as you would like. These are also the moments where you ask yourself, "Is this what I should be doing?" For me, everything around me could be crumbling, but the moment I get on the stage to perform, start playing with a great band, or write a song and record it, "music" reminds me why I love her.

Even through fatigue, frustration and anger, music brings a smile to my face. If this is not the feeling you have, if you can take it or leave it, my advice is that you keep searching. You will get to the point where you wish you were further along in your career, and making more money, where it seems like you are running up hill pulling a semi-truck. If you don't have the love, joy and passion for music, you will give up.

There is likely no book that will negate the fact that you have to work hard to achieve your goals. Talent is only a small part of the equation. Marketing and promotion, networking, image upkeep, touring and gigging, taking lessons and practicing, on top of paying bills, not neglecting your relationships, and other obligations are other parts of the equation. If you are not obsessed with this thing called music, please do yourself a favor and do something else.

To bring my emphasis to a close, until you are clear with what your specific goal may be in music, try different jobs. Don't be so scared to fail that you are paralyzed and do nothing. Find the thing that makes you the happiest and give yourself over to it, learning and doing it as much as you can. If you follow this advice, your life will be full of the things you love most.

"Once you know your worth, everyone else will too."

~.Andrae Alexander

How Do I Get Vocal Training?

Your voice is your product; I can't over emphasize how important it is to learn how to properly use it. Unless you have close relatives or friends that teach voice, finding vocal technique help for free might be difficult. Thankfully, with the internet (again), there are teachers and programs that can help you on your journey.

My first choice for vocal training would be for you to find an actual human teacher. Having a professional teacher with years of experience is the best way to go. Calling your local recording studio or instrumental music store is a great way to find teachers. Another great way is to go to your local college and speak with the vocal students and teachers there.

Understanding that budget may be a concern, instead of taking lessons from a professional teacher, start out with a student that has been taking lessons from the teacher you like. This way, you can learn the basics and learn the techniques of that particular teacher. You may be able to barter with the student for something other than money.

The next best thing to a teacher in the room with you is a recorded vocal coaching program. My favorite is the Arceneaux Approach. Eric Arceneaux has many years of vocal teaching experience, and offers a variety of lessons to purchase that will help with any vocal problem. His teaching style focuses on overall vocal health, which means it will translate well to any style or genre of music.

If buying his program is too expensive at this moment, check out his videos on *YouTube*™. Simply check out Eric Arceneaux on *YouTube*™ and subscribe to his channel. He has plenty of beginning lessons for free posted, and is willing to answer questions there as well.

Free isn't always the best thing, if you are really serious about making music your career. You need to invest in yourself. Why do you buy an expensive guitar? Because it has a sound that will enhance your overall performance. It's exactly the same with your voice. Investing in your music is just that, an investment that eventually will yield a return. Maybe it is difficult for you to pay for professional lessons, it's okay --that is why *YouTube*™ exists.

When you have the ability to invest in yourself, do it. You are your biggest asset, so, always bet on your success. In the end, when you sound better, you will be more marketable. Don't cut corners when it comes to you. If you absolutely have no money, then check out all the free resources online. However, having a vocal coach a few feet away from you is still the best option.

How Do I Get Confident With Performing?

If you ask most performers whether it becomes easier to get on stage and perform, they will tell you "yes." However, if you were to ask them if they still get nervous about getting on stage, the answer would be the same. Stage fright is something that you have to overcome, but that doesn't mean you won't have to deal with some anxiety.

I used to call the feeling of nervousness before a performance "stress." After talking to my friend Scotch Ellis Loring about it, I realized it was something else. He described the feeling as his body getting into a "high state of alert" before his show. It was great to hear another performer having a similar experience, and it changed the way I viewed this build-up of energy.

Every performer, including athletes, has this experience. However, for athletes, it is easier to understand why they need to be very alert. In this heightened state, their body performs at its very best, almost calling on their body's natural "fight or flight" reflexes. This same feeling translates to being in the "zone" for performers.

The "zone" is a high state of alertness, which allows you to remember song lyrics or ad-lib if you miss a word, remember dance steps, and have the energy to get an unresponsive audience out of their seats to

31

groove with you. The "zone" is the headspace where no matter what mistakes happens on the stage, you are alert enough to continue and make it a great performance.

Young or new performers don't understand that an audience paid to see a performance, and our job is to give them one at all costs. At the end of the day, if you are performing, you have to focus on one fact: people came to see you perform, so, take your time and give them the best you have at that moment.

The rush of energy that comes before a performance feels like "nervous energy," if you let it stay in your stomach. If you need to get the energy to go from "nervous energy" to "a high state of alert," you can do the following breathing exercise, which I have found quite helpful in the past.

I recommend doing this exercise when you have a moment to yourself before the show; your dressing room or a restroom will work. If you don't have a dressing room, and are too close to show time to go to a restroom, simply closing your eyes and doing this exercise anywhere will work. Let's get started.

HEART AND HEAD BREATHING EXERCISE:

1. Close your eyes and focus all of your attention on breathing deep, to what feels like the bottom of your stomach. Focus on the breath coming in and out of your body. Do this until you get the feeling of being totally in your body. Being content with your current circumstances is another way to describe the same feeling.

2. Focus your attention on the feeling in your stomach, and imagine it as a ball that your breath is flowing around.

3. With every breath, imagine that you are allowing the ball to slowly roll from your stomach to your heart.

4. Imagine that half of the ball is now at your heart, while the other half rolls further up to your head.

5. Circulate the energy from your heart and head.

Whenever you need to get back to feeling good and being focused on the moment you are in, do this exercise. I have done this exercise on stage; it's mostly deep breathing. You're going to be breathing anyway, you may as well make it deep.

I've discovered that another way to achieve the same results is by putting one hand on your heart and the other on your forehead. In this position, close your eyes, breathe deeply and imagine a feeling of light spinning at each point. If you are having trouble imagining the feeling of spinning, imagine a penny spinning at each point

From talking to performers who have horrible stage fright, I realized one thing that they all had in common, that is, they didn't perform in public enough. The best way to get over stage fright is to perform. As someone who is afraid of heights and of falling, I have made myself rock climb, go to the top of the Eiffel Tower, repel and even zip line over a forest. This has helped my fear of heights and of falling tremendously.

Facing your fear for the first time may be difficult, but it gets easier.. Am I still afraid? Yes! As a performer, you have to be honest with yourself. Is your love for performing greater than the fear and anxiety you have of performing? If your answer is "yes," then go perform. Make it a goal to perform as much as you can. Set a goal of performing at least fifty times and then reassess how fearful you are of performing.

Go to open-mic venues to perform, or go to your friends' parties and perform, or perform in the mirror to an imaginary crowd of thousands. The imaginary crowd will not count toward you goal of fifty performances, but it is better than doing nothing. You will only become comfortable performing if you take action.

Have fun; know that you are doing something you love, and do it with all the passion in the world. Give your audience an experience, and not just a show. Know that when you step on the stage, you own it. Know that every person in the audience came to see you (even if you're not the headliner performer). Take your time and give them all you have to offer, and you will be giving your best.

How Do I Get Photos and Videos Done?

Videos show how you interact with an audience and the actual energy of your shows. This will help in booking gigs. You can also use them in campaigns to get more fans, as well as for advertising of upcoming shows. The more good quality video you have, the bigger your video reel can be.

You will also need photos for album art and for your press kit. However, the question is "what is the best way to get your photos?". Once more, this solution has several options. You can start off by taking your own photos and editing them in *Photoshop™*, or a similar program. The fact that independent artists do everything for themselves, at least at first, turns them into master problem solvers.

To start, take hundreds of photos at the highest quality you can, and select the best photos. Technology is so advanced nowadays that most cameras, even the cameras on most mobile phones, are decent enough quality for great photos. After selecting your favorite photos, either hire a *Photoshop™* editor to make your photo the best that it can be, or obtain *Photoshop™* and do it yourself. Again, *YouTube™* has plenty of videos to teach you how to use *Photoshop™*.

A great site for inexpensive photo editors is *fiverr.com*. There, you can find an editor for five dollars to edit your photos and to even design flyers for you. I'll talk about outsourcing in more detail later in the book, but check out *fiverr.com* when you get a chance.

Whenever you have a show, always try to have someone take photos and video record. Like I said earlier, the photos and video footage can be used to make promotional videos, press kits, posters, artwork, and much more. Videos and photos tell the world that you are a serious and professional artist.

Of course, the best way to get great photos is to hire a professional photographer. When hiring a photographer, always look at their portfolio; you may even get ideas about how you want your photos to look. Going to a graphics design school or a photography school to find a photographer is also a great idea. Photographers and videographers need material to shoot, just as much as you need photos and videos; why not be available to them, as well?

Getting all of your friends to upload photos of your performance on your social media site is another great and free way to get photos. This way you can get a multitude of different angles. Seeing yourself from different angles will allow you to plan better shots in the future.

Also, make music videos, record yourself jamming, take photos of rehearsals, take photos of your after parties and so on. Get used to being in front of a camera and post the best photos and video to promote yourself. A professional photographer or videographer is always best, when you can't afford one, improvise and outsource.

WHAT IS OUTSOURCING?

In this day and age, the world is smaller than ever. The internet has allowed us to do things we could only dream of twenty years ago. You can reach the world in a fraction of a second, and you can become an instant success with the right tools and team, without leaving your house.

Outsourcing is not new to the business world, but it is new to most self-sustaining musicians. A huge benefit for you as a musician is the fact that you can hire someone in another part of the world, where the dollar is worth more. You can post a job and let the contractors bid for your job, sometimes making your out-of-pocket expense even lower.

What this means in even simpler terms: outsourcing gives you the same access to services at a lower cost than you would receive from the major labels. This includes access to website and graphic designers, marketing experts, public relations experts, social media experts, mixing and mastering engineers, bio writers, *Photoshop*™ editors, musicians, *Final Cut Pro*™ editors, merchandise designers, book editors, *Facebook*™ fan page creators, and most likely any other thing that doesn't require you to be there physically.

Here is a short list of outsourcing sites:

- _odesk.com_

- _elance.com_

- _freelancer.com_

- _peopleperhour.com_

- _guru.com_

- _fiverr.com_

Before posting and hiring for a job, be clear about what it is you want. For example, before looking for a publicist, make sure you are ready to be seen by everyone in the world. Do you have quality photos that are professionally edited? Is your website on par with major label artists? Does your _Facebook_™ page reflect you as the professional artist you define? Take the time to make sure that every aspect of who you are as an artist is the best quality you can make it in these avenues.

Don't think about each task as being separate from the other tasks that need to be done. Let's say, for example, you want to get a website built, so, you hire a great designer and build a great site. The next week you want to start selling CDs and T-shirts online, so, you hire a website designer to add a store to the site. To get people interested in your merchandise, you start a *Facebook*™ fan page and hire a designer to spruce it up, and again, call your website designer to add a link to *Facebook*™ on your website.

Everything that was done was needed. However, if you had taken a moment to think the process through, you could have paid the graphic designer and website designer once. Better yet, you could have found a website designer who was a graphic designer, and who also specialized in online store building with *Facebook*™ integration. Asking yourself, "What are my goals?" and "What do I need to do to reach my goals?" will save you time and money.

HOW DO I FUND A PROJECT?

Have you ever heard of the starving artist syndrome? It's when an artist focuses solely on his artistry, but gives no or very little energy to making his art profitable. The fact that you are an artist does not mean that you have to be poor; in fact, some of the richest people on this planet are artists. Why do so many artists go hungry or take jobs that they hate?

The reason so many artists are imprisoned in this lifestyle is due to the fact that they spend their time creating, but put little to no effort into actually promoting their creation. In my opinion, you have to give your 100 percent effort in creating the best product you can, and 100 percent effort in promoting it as well. If you lack in either area, you will fall short of your potential.

Now don't get me wrong, it's all fine and dandy that you want to spend most of your time creating, but if you're not generating income, you'll soon find out that eventually you'll have to choose between eating and creating; hence the "starving artist." Learning the "business" side of music is easier than most people think. Again, the internet provides so much access to good information that anyone with a question can find an answer.

Preparation is the key to fund a project with little money. The first thing you'll need to do is hire or gather musicians, unless you are a multi-instrument playing musician yourself. Once you have your musicians together, you should set time aside to practice before going into the studio. Being that you will most likely be your own producer, use this practice time to try out all of your ideas. Trying new ideas in the studio will cost you a lot of money.

As a producer, your job is to get the best performance from the musicians. Come into the rehearsal prepared and knowing what it is you want; this will set you apart as being great. Saying that, you have to be open to creativity, especially when you are dealing with good musicians. Never skip the rehearsal process, unless you have very experienced session musicians who record in the studio for a living. Failing to rehearse with inexperienced musicians will equal extra hours in the studio.

These days, recording equipment is very accessible. Instead of going a couple of times to a studio, you could always use that money to purchase your own recording equipment. This will eventually give you unlimited hours of recording, not to mention that you will be able to increase your general production knowledge.

A decent recording set-up should not cost you over $500. If you are a singer/songwriter with a decent computer, all you will really need is an audio interface (the device that converts sound into a digital format), music recording software, a condenser microphone, a couple of cables, and silence. To show you how simple this can be, I recently accessed *guitarcenter.com* and put together the following studio set-up:

1. Used MBOX mini- $129

2. Presonus Studio One 2.0 Producer Version- $199

3. MXL 990 Condenser Microphone- $59

4. Musician's Gear XLR 20' Microphone Cable- $14.99

Total: $401.99

If you check *craigslist.org*, you can find the gear you need, as well. My favorite thing to do is to complete an internet search of equipment that I want, and subsequently search for a slightly cheaper alternative. I then read as many reviews as I can handle before going to the music store to check out the equipment. Once I do this, I search the internet for deals on sites like *craigslist.org*, the used section of *guitarcenter.com*, or my favorite music store, Atomic Music (*atomicmusic.com*).

If you can't find musicians to help you to record, it would be a good idea to get a midi keyboard as well. This allows you to play your songs into the software using VSTi plug-ins. You can find a midi keyboard for about $69 brand new. VSTi's, for those who don't know, are Virtual instruments which can be played with a midi keyboard. This means that if you need to have a Cello in your song, you can use a VSTi plug-in and play the cello sound in your software.

By the way, another good place to track down musicians would be your local college or university. Generally, you will be able to track down some decent to pro musicians that would be willing to record for you for a pizza and maybe a couple of beers. If that's not your speed, I recommend church. Churches train some of the greatest musicians out there. Be creative in your search for musicians and find the music in your town. Where there is music, there will be musicians!

Another approach would be to check out all the major recording studios in the area that teach students the recording studio arts. The students require "test subjects," and may be able to record you at a discount, if you can get on the schedule. The benefit of this option is that you will have a quality product, and the experience of working at a great studio will be something you never forget. I had the privilege of working with students at the world renowned Omega Studios in Maryland,*www.omegastudios.com*. (They are amazing, and, please tell them that I sent you!)

Again, you should check out your local college, university or studio that may offer a course in studio engineering. Make friends with both the people teaching the courses and those taking the courses. The students will need projects to mix and master, which will both benefit you and the student alike. You could also use the internet to find someone to mix and master your music; I have found some for as low as $60 per song.

There is another method called "Crowd funding," which is probably the fastest way to make a large sum of money for your project. Websites like "*kickstarter.com*" and "*indiegogo.com*" allow you to create a fundraising campaign for free. You have to pay a percentage of the money generated, but that is a minimal fee. More importantly, you need to know how to reach the masses with your campaign. People generally don't mind donating money to a just cause. In order for these campaigns to work, you will need to "give" back to the people who are going to donate to your cause. What are things that you can give?

- CDs
- Merchandise

- Tickets to your shows
- Personal performances at their home
- Mentions on the CD album
- Posters
- A song written for them

You need to be able to motivate people through what you will offer them in return for their donation. Some people have made over $200k in a matter of a month to fund their creative endeavors; you just need to find the method that works for you. Crowd funding is one of the best ways that you could get the money you need for your project.

Don't see an obstacle as the end; continue to look for solutions. Be creative in your money-making efforts. Show people the value in what you do, give them a quality product, be likeable, give back in some way, and people will support you for life. Figure out if a recording studio or recording equipment is your best option; doing both it okay.

ANDRAE ALEXANDER

How Can I Get a Band Together?

As a musician, this subject is very touchy to me; I feel that musicians, as a whole, are undervalued already. The reason most artists need a band is to bring value to their show. Before I go into ways to find a band that will perform with you for little or no money, I need to state what I consider to be the obvious. Money is not the only way to pay for services.

Having a good band immediately takes a karaoke act to tour status within a few rehearsals. Knowing that, if you are a performer that is known for appreciating your band and bringing value to the individual members, you will always be able to find musicians who will work with you.

Showing your band that you appreciate and value them is very easy to do. For example, if you can't pay them what they are worth for a gig, at the very least, pay for parking and have a meal provided. Another thing you could do is to have thank you cards ready to hand out at the end of the gig, I learned that from Frank Sheffield, who is a great manager. Going the extra mile to show your appreciation will have musicians willing to work with you if a non-paying gig pops up.

Enough of that; let's get to finding musicians. We've covered certain hot spots for musicians earlier in this book, so, for the sake of not repeating myself, I'll simply provide a small list here:

- Music stores
- Recording studios
- Universities
- Music schools
- Music bars and cafes
- Personal ads
- Internet
- Church (Like I said, some of the best musicians come from church.)

When you take out a personal ad or an online ad, you want to be very specific. For example, if you are looking for a drummer for a teen polka rock group, the more specific you are, the better. You should put the age range desired of the musicians you want, (or how old you would like them to look), the style of music you want them to be able to play (maybe even reference specific musicians' names, "in the style of x drummer," for example), how they should dress, and any other information that is important to you.

The more specific you are, the higher your chances of finding the right musician. Don't forget to put in the ad how you plan on compensating the musicians, and their required experience. Just like you want the right musicians to audition for you, musicians want to audition for the right gigs: gigs that pay according to their skill and experience level.

One of my favorite places to place ads and search for gigs is *craigslist.org*. The "musicians" tab (community section), "TV / film / video" tab (jobs section) and the "talent" tab (gigs section) are my favorite places to find work. Being in LA, you would be very surprised at the quality of work you find for free on *craigslist.org*.

Personal Story:

> *My personal experience with this was shortly after I moved from Maryland to Los Angeles. I arrived in LA on May 1, 2009, checked craigslist.org on May 2nd, and saw an ad that said, "Looking for an African-American Jazz Pianist for a music video." I sent in a head shot, no music, just a head shot and was on the set of a music video with Kanye West on May 3rd, 2009. If you want to see the video, go to youtube.com and search "GLC ft. Kanye West 'Big Screen' - Official Video in HD". I am the piano player.*

Another option for acquiring musicians is by going to music stores where they teach lessons and asking some of the students as they walk in to their lesson if they are interested in doing a gig. That sounds desperate, but you have to do what you have to do sometimes.

If all of this fails, start a band where you are a member. If you put a band together where you all share everything equally, you are more likely to have members that are willing to do free gigs to get started. No matter where you are, I guarantee there are musicians wanting to gig. Where there is a will...there is a band! Don't stop until you find them!

What is a Producer?

We've been talking about producers, but let's jump into a deeper understanding about what a producer does. In essence, look at him like the general project manager. It is the producer's job to produce a song that sounds like a finished product. Saying that, there are two main types of producers: producers that are musicians and producers that aren't musicians, but have the gift to hear and communicate their ideas to musicians.

As a lover of great music, I don't care which type of producer you are or choose to work with, just as long as he or she can deliver a great product. The producer can be an engineer that gives you advice on what to do to make your song sound better. Engineers make great producers. Because of their long hours in the studio hearing session after session, they know tricks to making your song sound good.

Of course, musicians that have experience leading a band tend to be great producers. They have musical knowledge and the leadership skills needed to run a studio session and keep everything on schedule. At times, you'll hate your producer (especially in the studio), but in the end, you should love him or her for the finished product.

As an artist, you hire a producer to allow you to focus on your performance in the studio. It is the producer's responsibility to focus on everything and everyone else. He will handle scheduling of musicians and studio sessions, keeping the session on schedule, keeping you calm, and getting a great performance from everyone involved in the session.

Another skill to look for in a producer, or even learn yourself, is knowledge of studio recording software. Having this skill will give you the ability to know when an engineer is purposefully going slow to add more hours onto the studio session. This is not a common practice among engineers, but there are some that do this to unknowledgeable artists.

A producer has many faces, but when it comes to producing your music, you need to find someone you trust musically. Obviously, you will always keep the creative control over the music, but a great producer can definitely help you reach a level that supersedes your own musical expectations and understanding.

How Do I Find Music Professionals?

Networking is one of the skills that you as an artist will have to develop quickly. Networking is a skill you need to perfect in order to achieve bigger projects and goals. Once you have a decent grasp of networking, where do you go to practice and use your networking skills?

You should practice networking everywhere, all of the time. I have a friend who is very outgoing. In ten minutes of being in a room, he has met and is friends with everyone there. Using him as an example, you can practice networking anywhere at any time. Getting comfortable talking to people you don't know is the key to successful networking. To practice, take the time to ask the teller about her day, ask the postman how his route is going today; basically, talk to anyone who will have a conversation with you.

Once you are comfortable talking to people you don't know, go to where musicians are and befriend everyone. Bars, clubs, and music stores are a great place to start. Don't just focus on musicians, having friends or associates that own a bar, book the acts at a club, and promote for performance venues are all beneficial friends or associates.

Another way to connect to other music industry professionals is by using the internet (again). There are also thousands of musicians and producers to be found online. *Twitter*™, *Facebook*™ and *LinkedIn*™ have over one billion people using them. If you do a search for "music producer," "sound engineer," "photographer," "promoter," or whatever service you need, you may be surprised to find out how many people to which you can connect.

Follow these people, and some of them will also follow you. Have a game plan, know what it is you need, as well as what you have to offer. Nobody wants to waste time or energy on something that will not benefit them, so, it is important to know what these benefits are for others before you pitch an idea. Always know that you have something to offer, and go into every situation with this knowledge.

The first time you meet any of these individuals, try not to talk too much about what you have planned, and primarily focus on creating bonds between the person and you. Once you have established a relationship and a bit more trust, then, you can let them in on your plan. Make sure you provide benefit to your new connection first, before trying to benefit from the relationship yourself.

Recap of places to find music connections:

- Music bars

- Clubs (where they play live music or have a DJ; DJs are great connections)

- Open mic nights

- Facebook™

- *YouTube™*

- Colleges

- Recording studios

- Music stores

- Churches

- Anywhere there is music

On a budget, you'll probably find that the best place to network is your local college. College students are more willing to work with your budget than a seasoned professional musician, photographer or graphic designer. In some cases, you can find wonderful talent that might work for food.

How Do I Find a Producer in a Small Town?

So, maybe you live in a town that doesn't have a big music scene - what to do? In the spirit of musicians from all ages, it's time to hit the road, and go to "the city." Almost every mid-sized to large city in the United States has an open mic night, a spot for jam sessions, recording studios, or even karaoke bars. In these venues, you will find singers, musicians, and producers. Using your networking skills, you can find whomever you want.

If you happen to not find any producers at a certain venue, talk to the singers or musicians present. Just about every musician knows where the other musicians hang. If you don't have any luck through this route, go to church. Almost every church has musicians, especially churches that are predominately African-American. If you look at the musicians that play for and tour with your favorite artists, no matter what genre of music, you will most likely find church musicians.

Be relaxed and work on creating a relationship with the person, before you start talking about the "business of you." When people are at a bar or venue, and they are spectators, assume that they are "not available" for business at that time; they are likely enjoying the night off. Instead, focus the conversation on "getting to know the person," as if you were meeting a new acquaintance and building a friendship.

This is what we call "building rapport," which basically means, "building trust" with a person. By the end of the night, the producer or musician should think of you as a "nice person, friendly, cool, fun" and so on. Be sure to get their information at the end of the night, before heading home.

When you call them to see if they want to record, be sure to remind them of who you are: that "nice person that is friendly, cool, and fun." This should act as a good icebreaker, and will gain you access to more contacts and resources to help your goal.

Another approach you can take, if you still haven't found anyone to help you record, is to find out where the nearest recording studio is located. Even if you can't afford to record there, you can "network" with some of the producers there that might be able to direct you to a more affordable solution, that is, a producer that fits your budget. In addition to this, recording studios generally have a lot of contacts within the music industry, and would most likely be able to help you in other areas, as well. Just remember that you are that "nice *talented* person that is friendly, cool, and fun" every time you meet people. If you are going to a recording studio, you can be slightly more to the point, but it's always a good idea to be the most likeable you, especially when meeting new people.

If you have no luck with the recording studio, go to the nearest music stores. Music stores are full of musicians who are very knowledgeable about the local music scene. In my experience, they are also full of great producers and very skilled musicians, as well.

If all of these locations yield no results, go on the internet. *Facebook™, Craigslist™, YouTube™,* and any of the outsourcing sites will give you results. You'll be surprised how many musicians you can find on *fiverr.com* to sing a demo for you. Start your search for music producers or musicians in your area, then slowly work your way out to nearby cities. The fact that you are trying to do music in your area most likely means that there are a few other people in your area trying to do the same thing.

If there is absolutely no way for you to track down a producer, become one! Depending on what you want to achieve, you may need to adapt your game plan. If you do decide to go this route, be prepared to study and watch videos until you get the gist of things. If this is your passion, don't let anything stop you from doing it. The best advice I can give: do the best with what you have at this moment, and enjoy the ride. Make sure you allow no obstacle to prevent you from moving forward.

ANDRAE ALEXANDER

"The best advice I can give: do the best with what you have at this moment, and enjoy the ride."

~Andrae Alexander~

I Found a Producer, Now What?

Before approaching a producer, you need to be clear on a couple things, or you'll sound like a kid with a dream, as opposed to a serious artist on a mission. You will need to know how much money you are willing to spend on production, as well as how many songs you want produced. These are the most important factors, but what if you don't have a penny to your name?

This is where your good looks and charming smile will come into play, that, and a word. The word is "Collab" or "collaboration." It is the secret artists' codeword for, "Hey, you see these flies coming out of my pockets? Is there any way you can find it in your heart to work with me for free, oh great and illustrious one of infinite creativity!" If the producer is new to producing and trying to build his catalog, you might be able to mutually benefit by collaborating. If the producer is a bit more on the experienced side, it might be more difficult.

The music industry is almost like high school. If you are the new kid on the block, then you can't simply just walk up and be "cool," you have to offer something. This could, and should, be your talent and skill. If you are still developing your talent and skill, but still have the desire to be successful, you will probably have to offer your time, and possibly services other than music to get producers or musicians to work with you. For example you can offer to organize their studio, do secretarial work, or some other creative idea.

Do research on the producer before you talk to him, and mention that you know his or her work. Also, remember that people are more willing to trust someone they see on a regular basis; so, try to show up at the spots where all the musicians go, and make genuine friends. With friends in the industry, it is a lot easier to achieve your career goals. You will also have access to a wealth of experience and knowledge from your newfound friends.

Keeping in mind that the music industry is like high school, when you go to these musical "watering holes," you should always dress for success. The name of the game is "appearance," which means that you should always look and feel like the successful artist you are becoming. If you look like a million bucks, people will automatically assume that is your worth. They don't know you; they don't know your economic situation or your experience level, until you tell them or show them.

This does not mean to take out a loan to buy the latest clothes, this just means to look your best. When you are at your best, you feel good about yourself, and people will feel that from you. At the same time, you can't just rely on looks alone; you need to be able to back up your appearances. Be friendly, but don't try to impress them with your knowledge of the industry, especially if you don't have any.

When you hear a conversation about an aspect of the music industry that you don't know much about, it is better to keep quiet and listen, than open your mouth and show your ignorance. If you tell everybody that you are a producer, but have never been in a studio before, music industry professionals will know. It's okay to not know everything, it's not okay to act like you do.

If you want to become a producer, I would advise you to get some equipment and do some work "pro bono," to obtain some experience. Once you have the basics down, you can start networking, and will actually know something about the profession. In addition to gaining experience, you will also be giving a helping hand to other musicians, which, if you believe in it or not, is a very good thing. If you reap what you sow, which you do, just as you helped someone with what you can offer, you will also be helped in the same manner.

This doesn't mean that you should always do things for free, but use your first initial encounters as learning opportunities, and when you feel competent enough to actually start charging, go for it. Until then, experience and knowledge is better than any dollar amount you can receive.

As an independent artist, it is essential to make "allies" along the way, because unlike mainstream artists, you won't have a billion dollar corporation backing you up. Luckily, you're not alone, because in the indie scene, there are an abundance of people wanting to use their talent. They need you to practice on to gain the experience that will lead them to their dream job; you need them for the same. Surround yourself with people as talented as or more talented than you, and then work together. You'll learn to do things better, have people who will back you up when you need it, and vice versa.

As a Producer, How Can I Grow?

Music producers, no matter how talented, want to know how to get to "the next level." This usually means the level where you can eat food, pay bills, and make music and money, all at the same time. This sounds easy, but the practical application eludes most of us. Experience, Excellence and Exposure are our best friends in the journey to success, which I call, "The Three E's."

One of the down falls of most producers is that they don't have a realistic view of their talent level. Thinking you have learned all that there is about producing is the fastest way to becoming dated in your sound. Also, just because you are the best in your circle, does not mean you are the best. Study your peers, and not just peers in your area. If you live in New York, find some of your peers on the West Coast. There are phenomenally talented music producers all over the world; don't live in a bubble.

Listen to styles of music that you wouldn't typically listen to for inspiration. Just because you are an R&B producer, doesn't mean you can't learn something from a Rock producer. No I.D., one of the most influential producers of our time, once said to me, "The difference between a good producer and a great producer is that a great producer doesn't stop until the music is exactly how he hears it."

I don't think it can get any simpler than that!

The way you prove your "Experience" is by having a catalog of great music. Your first goal should not be to have thousands of tracks on your hard drive; that's fine, but the producer who networked, found songwriters to write over his music, and has only a hundred completed songs, will always win over you. He has shown his experience in making tracks and finishing songs.

Don't be afraid to do work for free to get completed songs. Artists will have more faith in you and be willing to pay you more, with proof of your ability to complete full songs. Laying this foundation will not only give you complete songs for your catalog, it will also give you more confidence in your ability to work with singers, as well as finish projects.

On the subject of "Excellence," I have to say, that getting a musical education is the fastest route. Finding a teacher that can show you where you need to improve, and give you techniques to improve, is important. As a producer, we need multiple teachers: instrument, voice, mixing, and music theory teachers, to name just a few.

I understand that money may be a factor in how many teachers you think you can afford. Being a producer, use your talent to barter. Find a great vocalist, and offer music production. If that doesn't work, use the internet. In this information age, *YouTube™*

has become a surrogate teacher to many of us.

Another piece to excellence is staying current. Technologically, you need to stay current with trends in mixing, sound choices, and even updated equipment. Being friends with other producers, and seeing how they use the same equipment as you, is also a great way to grow. Cultivating these friendships can lead to more work for you, as well. Everyone needs someone they can pass work to, just make sure to return the favor.

This leads me to the final piece that just about everyone misses, "Exposure." The best advice I can offer is to plant what you want people to see. To be more clear:

1. **Have a decent website with your current resume'**. Taking jobs for free or for an extremely discounted rate will help you build your resume'.

2. **Get as many write-ups as you can.** Writing press releases about your current projects, getting friends who have blogs to write about you, volunteering for a worthwhile cause, and posting photos on social media sites will all help. Make sure that all of this is on your website as well; think of your website as your home base, and you want everyone to go there.

3. **Hire help to get noticed.** The first thing most people think is that getting someone else to help is expensive. Not in this day and age where the internet has made the world a smaller place. Using outsourcing sites like *fiverr.com* (again) to find marketing help for $5 is common practice now-a-days. (You're welcome!)

To sum this question up, you need to put in the work, to build your career. Thinking that your talent alone will get you where you need to go is unrealistic, but being clear about who you want to be as a producer/artist/musician, and starting to operate on that level now, is how you succeed.

"If you don't give yourself to your music, it's not a passion, it's a hobby."

~Andrae Alexander

What is Mixing and Mastering, Do I Need It?

Before I answer the first part of this question, I will answer the second part - "YES!" As I continue to explain mixing and mastering, you'll begin to understand why you definitely DO need it.

When you record audio, you can hear that every instrument has its own frequency range. For instance, the voice has a certain range within the sonic spectrum that is very different from the drums. The main job of mixing is to make sure you can hear every sound in the song clearly. Visually, the equivalent is like walking into an organized closet; nothing is cluttered, and you can see everything.

You don't want a song that has overpowering drums and a weak sounding vocal performance, or vice versa. That is where sound mixing comes in to play, that is, making sure every sound in the song fits to make the whole song sound great. Making sure the volume of every sound compliments each other is the first step. Volume gives the effect of the sound being close to you or away from you. Loud being close, and soft being away.

After that, panning is used. Panning is where you have a sound louder in the right or left side of the speaker. For example, listen to your favorite song in earphones, listen to what sounds you hear in either side of the earphones. Panning is one way for listeners to be able to distinguish between the sounds in the song.

Equalizing is another technique used. Equalizing, or EQing, is up and down in frequency. Listen again to your favorite song; listen for where the kick drum sits in the music. Listen again to see where the strings or guitar sit in the song. Strings seem high and the bass seems low.

Having a decent grasp of these techniques will allow you to be able to place a sound just about anywhere in the mix. After you have a good mix, you need to "master" the song. The mixing engineer works with the individual sounds of the song to mix them together, the mastering engineer works with the song as a whole.

There are a few things that mastering does to a song. One big thing is to make sure your song is as loud as it can be without distorting the sound. When making a CD, there could have been more than one mixing engineer. The mastering engineer will EQ all of the songs to make it sound like they should be on a CD together.

Most mixing engineers will know a mastering engineer, or even be able to do it themselves. I have also had great success with an online mastering company, "Diamond Disc Audio," they are out of Nashville, _diamonddiscaudio.com_. (Please tell Doug I said hello; he has quick turn-a-rounds, and great prices.)

Mixing and mastering is one of the things that separate amateurs from professionals. I can't stress this enough, never skip these steps or leave the process of mixing and mastering your music in the hands of an amateur!

How Do I Get My Songs Mixed?

Mixing your song is just as important, if not more so, as recording a great performance of your song. It doesn't matter if you can solo like Jimi Hendrix, or play drums like Carter Beauford, if it doesn't sonically sound good. A good mixing engineer can make a decent song sound like a great song; this is a step you shouldn't rush through.

If you've been taking my advice so far, you should have already networked and made friends with a few musicians/producers. After you have recorded your songs, now would be the time to call your friends for recommendations about mixing engineers; every professional music maker has their favorites.

One of my favorite producers/mixing engineers is Matty Trump. You can contact him at mixandmastermysong.com. He does mixing and mastering as well as produces great music; tell him I said hi.

If you still haven't connected with any musicians who can suggest a good engineer, here are some other options. Again, go to your nearest college or university that has music engineering courses. Most of the students in these programs need music to practice their mixing skills; why not let them practice on your music? In most cases, they will do it for free, or for a nominal fee. You can also take out a personal ad on *Craigslist™, Facebook™ and Twitter™*.

> **"Not having money is an excuse that keeps most people from pursuing their dream. Be persistent and knock on every door until one opens."**
>
> **~Andrae Alexander**

If you have exhausted all of your resources and still can't find an engineer, invest in the equipment and do it yourself. *YouTube™* has plenty of free videos which teach you basic and advanced mixing techniques; don't let anything stop you from completing your goals.

There is one rule in music: if it sounds good, then, it is good. So, get that album mixed either by a pro, a friend, or do it yourself. Test it on your computer speakers and your car speakers to be sure that it sounds good. Take your time on this step, and do it right the first time, you will thank me later.

What is a Manager, When Do I Need One?

Managers act as the "hands" of the band behind the scenes. A manager finds work for you as an artist, negotiates deals, collects money, and takes care of you. In essence, the manager is an extension of the band that will do all the dirty work. The band's responsibility is to create new music, to perfect their show and music. The manager does all the rest.

A manager's fee is between 10-20 percent of your salary as an artist; this means he or she gets paid when you get paid. There are some managers that will pay for studio time and other expenses;, make sure there is a contract stating what those expenses may be, and how the manager is to be reimbursed. Make sure you have an entertainment lawyer look over the contract to explain clearly what it means.

Never give up complete control of your career to anyone; everyone, including managers, work for you, and can be replaced. Go into the relationship knowing what you want, and be clear. Starting off with a trial period before signing a long-term agreement is a smart decision.

A good question to ask yourself: "Should I get a manager or should I self-manage?" A lot of artists really are perplexed with this question. These days, there are so many viable online solutions that make a manager unnecessary, until you have established yourself as an artist.

Having a manager means receiving less money, but it also means doing less work in managing the business side of your career. The thought of less money may sound scary, but if you have an experienced manager who will work to get you paid, you will ultimately make more money. Another benefit is having someone else fight your battles.

One of the jobs of a manger is to get money that is owed to you from gigs. The manager not only negotiates on your behalf, he or she makes sure you have everything that you need to make you feel comfortable and able to perform at your highest level. A manager is almost like hiring a baby sitter for yourself. He or she speaks, negotiates, hires and fires on your behalf; your happiness and best good in every situation is the manager's priority. Having someone this involved in your life and business is a decision that you shouldn't take lightly.

The goals you have set for your career will determine whether or not you need a manager. If your goal is to play more local club dates and sell your CD online, you probably don't need a manager. You can go to clubs and hand them a package yourself; you can also find out how much to ask for by befriending some local musicians. You may need a manager, if your goal is to get better paying shows and tour to promote your CD.

You don't need a manager, if you don't have a decent foundation. If you are a musician, but have no recorded music and no gigs coming up, you don't need a manager. What would there be for the manager to manage? Some artists think that their talent alone is sufficient, and they should be given gigs immediately. Just like anything else, there is an industry standard.

Recording in a studio allows you to develop your sound as an artist and proves to the rest of the world that you are at a decent level to perform. Don't skip this step. Put in the work to get it done. You have to put in the work to get yourself as far as you can with what knowledge you have. This sounds simple, but is a huge concept for some to grasp. After you have your goals clearly written, start working. Once you have done all that you know how to do, you will be at a point where you can assess whether or not you need a manager.

When you meet a manager and they ask you about yourself, you'll be taken more seriously, if you can clearly explain what you have already done, and what it is you want. If you expect someone to work for you, you have to show that you already work hard for yourself.

When most artists say that they want a manager, they really want a booking agent, that is, someone to get them gigs. Unlike a manager who gets about 20% of your income as an artist, a booking agent only gets paid when he gets you gigs. A good booking agent has relationships with a decent amount of venues. There are booking agents and agencies all over the world that need artists to place at different venues. Just like with a manager, if you have no music to let them hear, and no fans, you are probably not going to get the results you are looking for.

What is Publishing?

Publishing is not difficult to understand. A song has two equal parts to it, the writer of the song and the publisher of the song. The writer of the song actually created the song. The publisher is the entity that controls who can use the song, collects and distributes the money (royalties) that the song generates, and is responsible for getting the song licensed.

When a song is played on the radio, both the writer and the publisher get paid. The writer's portion is 50 percent of the song, the publisher's portion is the other 50 percent. For example, if there is one writer of a song and two publishers of the same song, the writer gets fifty percent and the publishers have to split the other fifty percent. As a writer, you can own your own publishing company, which will entitle you to one hundred percent of the royalties from your song.

In order to collect your royalties from writing and publishing, you must:

1. Register with a PRO (performance rights organizations). ASCAP, BMI, OR SESAC are the three we use in the U.S. In order to register as a publisher, you have to have a song that is released or being released. Being "released" simply

means making your music available for purchase.

2. Once you are registered with a PRO as a publisher, you need to start a business with the same name as the publishing name that you registered. For this reason, it is smart to do research before picking a name. For most independent musicians, I recommend LLCs. Do the research and figure out which one is best for you.

3. Subsequently, open a bank account to be able to cash the checks that the PRO sends.

A cheaper alternative is to file a DBA (Doing Business As) form. This will allow you to cash the checks using the accounts you already have.

After all of this is done, you can now copyright your songs with the Library of Congress, U.S. Copyright Office, in Washington, DC (*copyright.gov*), as a writer and publisher. This is really simple, and costs about thirty dollars to do. Copyrighting your songs protects them from being stolen. (It is imperative that you have your work copyrighted before sharing it with anyone.)

If you didn't understand all of that, I'll say it all again in a slightly different way. You write a song (writer), and the publisher of the song controls who can use the song and collects money on behalf of the writer and publisher of the song. People who want to use your song know what publisher to contact by who files at the Copyright Office.

Before I move on, I want to touch on another topic that pertains to filing at the Copyright Office. If you own a record label or are executive producer of a song, which means you are paying for the song to be recorded, you file the SR (sound recording) form with the Copyright Office. This means that if anyone wants to use the already recorded version of the song, you get paid royalties. If you are the writer or publisher of the song, you file the PA (performing arts) form. This means you own the song. This allows you to collect royalties every time any one uses your song no matter how many people record different versions of it.

WHAT ARE ROYALTIES, HOW DO I GET THEM?

I am going to start at the beginning, and walk you through royalties. By the end of this paragraph you are going to love me even more. So, the moment you write a song, you own it; this song is your property. Unlike property you see physically, like a bike or house, this property is called "intellectual property." When you own intellectual property and register it with the Copyright Office, you now own the copyright. When someone wants to sing your song on their CD, TV show, or put your song in a movie, they find out who owns the copyright, and gets his or her permission to use the song. They pay you every time the song airs, sells, or is performed. The payment is called royalties.

As you see, this is not a hard concept. Using the basic knowledge you now have, I want to add a few more concepts that will give you a greater understanding of how royalties and ownership of a song works.

As you now know, ownership of a song has two parts to it:

1. 1.The person or people who wrote the song with lyrics and melodies

2. The publisher who controls who has permission to use the song

The writer and the publisher split any money made from the song equally. Some people tell me they don't think this is fair, saying that the creators of the song should get a bigger share. I believe that these people don't truly understand the importance and great advantage of having a good publisher.

After a great song is written, if there is no one there to promote the song to music supervisors or recording artists to use the song, the song would sit on a computer, with no one to hear it. Both the writer and the publisher doing their jobs well are needed to make money from the song.

The great thing about this system is that a writer can also be a publisher by joining a PRO, themselves. Again, PROs are responsible for getting you money when your song is performed - this means CD sales, TV and radio performances, as well as performances in live venues. Again, the PROs in the U.S. are ASCAP, BMI and SESAC.

When you fill out the application to join a PRO, you are asked if you are joining as a writer or publisher. If you want to be a publisher as well as a writer, fill out both applications. For more details about the requirements for joining as a publisher, go to the PRO website you are interested in joining, they are very clear about the requirements.

Once you are registered with a PRO, you have to "license" your music in order to be able to collect royalties. A license is just you giving permission for your song to be used by someone other than yourself. There are a few licenses that you can give, they are:

1. **Mechanical License** - you are paid a royalty from physical CDs and your music being distributed.

2. **Compulsory Mechanical License** - a third party doesn't ask your permission to record your song, however they pay the Mechanical Licensing Rates established by copyright law. You can call the Harry Fox Agency to find out rates. They are a great resource, and will handle finding copyright owners, and answer paperwork questions for you.

3. **Sync License** - you are paid a royalty if your song is used with visual images, for example, if placed in a film or television show.

4. **Performance License -** you are paid from your PRO when someone performs your song. This license is offered to businesses and venues. This also covers radio play, as well as if someone performs your song live on TV.

5. **Digital Performance Licensing** - you are paid from Sound Exchange for your song

being played on digital transmission (satellite radio, internet radio, etc.)

6. Print Music License - you are paid a royalty when someone buys your song in sheet music form.

If you look at the definitions of each license, you can see exactly how money is made on a song. To say it differently, money is made from your song by:

1. Putting the song on a CD (or any other device for audio including online downloads) and selling it.

2. Having your song played on the radio on a consistent basis.

3. Having your song in films and/or TV shows.

4. Performing your song at venues associated with PROs.

5. Having your song played on satellite and Internet radio stations on a consistent basis.

6.   Having your music written out as sheet music and selling it.

As the creator of the song, you don't need to give yourself a license to use it in any of these ways. You just need to know that these are the current ways money is made from a song. The great thing about being an independent artist is that you can be creative and try anything you want to promote yourself and get your music out using these six methods.

A fairly new development: websites that act very similar to live concerts, charging the audience a fee to watch the show as you perform. While you perform, ads for your CD and other merchandise are constantly being offered to the audience. In my opinion, this is the next wave that indie artist should jump on. Think about it -- this is the TV and computer monitor generation.

The fact that you are probably reading this on an eBook reader or your computer is testament to this fact. I suggest you get your products as professional as you can possibly make them, and jump on this wave, before it gets to be common knowledge. It's a lot of work being creative and having to find avenues for your song to make money, as well. A great writer/publisher relationship can be great for all involved. Saying that, being able to collect all of the revenue that's generated by your song is great too, it just takes a bit more work, if you are doing it alone. Don't worry, you are an indie artist though, so, you were built to persevere.

HOW DO I SELL MYSELF AS AN ARTIST?

This is probably one of the most important questions out there -- how to sell yourself. The reason this is important is simple; people buy from people they like. You probably don't eat at McDonalds because it's the best, you likely can find hundreds of other burgers that are better. You eat there because of the memories and good feelings associated with it. Having said that, people buy your music, t-shirts and buttons, because they like you.

The first and most important aspect that you need to have down is a strong belief in yourself. If you are not convinced that you are an artist, then nobody else will either. The great singer and artist YahZarah said to me once, "If you don't believe you belong in the room, then no one else will". This doesn't mean to act like something you're not. On the contrary, be your best and authentic self at all times.

If you feel you were born to perform and sing, give yourself over to your artistry. Someone who "dabbles" at performing will never be as great as the person who is consumed with his or her artistry. People can sense an actor, someone mimicking another artist. If you truly are an artist, all you have to do is fully embrace and be your authentic artistic self. This is the first step to "selling" yourself.

87

Besides money and exposure, what's the difference between a famous artist and yourself? Typically, the answer is simple: confidence. Confidence in you yourself and your abilities is the first internal line that needs to be crossed. Well known artists have the social proof of their ability and the fans to assure them of their greatness.

"Before anyone else tells you you're great, know you are great."

~Andrae Alexander

Be clear about what you're selling. If you're not clear about who you are as an artist, how can you properly market and brand yourself to the people who would love your artistry? Imagine going to the store to buy cereal, and after purchasing the box of cereal, you open it to find popcorn. You would probably feel disappointed and even deceived. Save yourself time and frustration by knowing who you are as an artist.

Now that we have established that, you need to start working on building social proof. People want to be "in the know." They don't like to feel like they are the last to know something. Drawing on this fact is simple. Being active and amassing a large number of followers, friends, and fans on social media is a great way to get more of the same.

Get as many people talking about you as possible. I'll go into more detail on how to do this, but for now, I'll say, get written up in blogs, magazines, newspapers and anywhere else potential fans may find you. When fans find you and start to "follow" you, always show appreciation. Don't treat social media like an infomercial; that's the fastest way to lose fans. Actually being social and authentically interactive with them will win you fans for life.

Finally, you must always evolve in your craft. As people, we find ourselves in a constant state of evolution. Our experiences and daily interactions shape our perception. Your talents should always grow; know that there is always room for improvement. By maintaining this mentality, you will become the artist you dream of being. The fact is, you already are that artist; you just need to make everyone else realize it.

Your music career has as much potential as you want it to have, and I'm showing you how to get there, what tools to use, how to get fans, how to network, how to plan, and much more. The action is all up to you; you need to put in the effort to get the results you desire.

How Do I Network?

Networking in essence is nothing more than effective and planned communication. It's all about meeting people, making noise and creating contacts. For some people, networking comes natural, they effortlessly make new contacts and easily connect with people of influence. For some of us, it might be a bit more difficult, but with practice, it can become second nature.

There are certain concepts that you need to understand before we start. The first concept that needs to be addressed is "being authentic and prepared". Essentially, when you network, you'll be promoting yourself, that is, selling the idea that you are an artist, producer or whatever you choose to be. The relationships you build could become essential for you to achieve success within the industry, or at the very least, give you the experience and confidence to approach the person who will help your career along.

Being authentic and prepared is a very simple concept. You will take what you have achieved so far and make it look as good as you possibly can. For example, if you don't have a finished CD and don't really perform out too much, you may have photos from your performances. If you want to get more places to perform, you can at least have a website that has the photos you do have with details of your performances posted. This will show that you are working.

Before we move on, take a moment to think about what resources and people you need to meet to help you in your career. For example, if you are a singer, you may need a producer, or even a photographer. Think about what you can do now to prepare for when you meet these people. Ask yourself this question, "What can I do now to make myself look more prepared?" Answer this question, and start doing the work to prepare for your inevitable meeting.

The trick to networking comes down to how you are perceived by the people you meet. You will obviously be meeting new people, and in many cases, you'll have to initiate the conversation. If you are someone who fears talking to people, I'm going to give you a few tips to help you seem confident. You will never become a huge raving success by yourself; understand that people are resources, and that you need to learn how to work with them.

One of the hardest things to do is deal with yourself. It's a known fact that people are attracted to confident and happy people. Become one of those people, and half of the battle is already won. Being confident and happy is easier said than done, so, let me give you three tips that will help you while you work on actually being happy and confident.

1. The first thing people notice is your eyes. Don't make the mistake of looking around while talking to someone. This makes it seem like you don't really want to talk to this person, or that you're not sincere. When meeting someone, keep eye contact until you know his or her name and eye color. This may seem strange for some, but this makes people feel like you are paying attention to them. When you talk to them you shouldn't just stare at their eyes, because that too can be awkward. I recommend looking at their eyes, and then their mouth for a few seconds, and then back to their eyes again. This makes you seem interested. Although, you really should be interested; It should never be only about you.

2. Smile! Smiling makes you look more attractive and inviting. Don't just smile with your mouth; learn to smile with your whole face. To practice this, wait until you are genuinely happy and smiling already. Go look at yourself in a mirror, even take a picture. Feel how your face feels. What muscles do you

feel working? When you smile from now on, try to recreate this moment.

3. Shaking hands is an art form to which you should pay attention. If you are a man shaking another man's hand, it is generally expected that you give a nice firm handshake. Firm does not mean bone crushing. To get a good grasp of what equates as a nice firm grip, shake hands with your friends and ask them what they think. Another thing to address is a man shaking the hand of a woman. In corporate settings, women tend to have strong grips, however, everywhere else, women tend to have a softer grip than most men. Gentlemen, to make sure you don't give too much pressure, slow your squeeze down slightly until you feel her stop squeezing.

Now that you are talking to someone, what do you talk about? The point of the conversation is to see if and how you both can benefit from each other. Once you figure it out, talk about it. I try not to go straight to questions like, "what do you do." This makes it seem like you are not really trying to develop a relationship that is mutually beneficial for both of you. A better way to approach the conversation is by talking about what is going on at that moment.

For example, let's say you are at an open mic watching musicians perform. Comment on the band or how great the wings taste. This will immediately place you in friend status, which is a much better place to be. After a while of talking, you can bring up what you do and gain a possible connection. The key here is always letting the other person talk more than you talk. Ask questions, listen to the responses, and comment on them.

After the conversation, you have to be able to stay in touch with this person. You hopefully have figured out how this connection can benefit the both of you. Now get to the point and get their number and email address. You can do this by saying, "It's been great talking to you, do you mind if I contact you later to continue our discussion?" or "Hey, I'm new to the music scene here, do you mind if I call you to ask your advice on how I can get connected?"

After receiving their contact information, I like to follow up by sending an email or text, possibly both within one or two days of meeting the person. In the email or text, I put my first and last name, where we met, and a brief reminder of the conversation. For example,

Hi John, this is Andrae Alexander. We met at Bill's jam session on Wednesday. Thanks for the advice on how to meet more people. I've already seen great results! I remember you said that you needed a music producer for several artists that you manage. I've attached my bio, along with a few links to examples of my work. When are you available to talk about this further?

Andrae

It is necessary to make a habit out of networking; knock on every door and never give up. You never know when or where you will find the keys to success, or more importantly, who's holding the keys. Networking also means playing out as much as you can. If you have to go to open-mics and jam sessions, or even take a few free gigs to accomplish this, then do it.

Not only will you gain more experience, performing will put you in front of more people that you can talk to, and gives you a reason to approach and be approached by people. Treat every gig like your one time opportunity to show what you're made of to the world. Always treat everybody with respect, even the cleaning crew. You are always being watched, and you also never know who the people that are watching you know. As long as you are personable and talented, it's just a matter of time.

I know a lot of people who use business cards, to me this is less personable. Get their number in your phone and your number in theirs. I will literally hand a person my phone and take theirs to exchange contact information. While I'm on this topic, a cool app that I use is "bump". You can use it to bump phones with another person who has "bump" and you both will have each other's info stored in your phones automatically.

Let's move on to a scenario that is inevitable in the entertainment industry. You have just met a person who can literally make a phone call and help your career, or maybe even give you the gig of your dreams. You have the best conversation with the person, and even exchange contact information. A few days go by and you are still waiting to be contacted by this person who made it seem like this gig for you was a sure thing. You call them to either be ignored or brushed off. This has happened to everyone, so don't feel too bad.

The first time it happens is the worse, in my opinion, because no one warns you of it. Earlier in my career, I took it personally, but now I have realized that it is not altogether a bad thing. I'll tell you why; most people who get brushed off enough give up and tell the world horror stories of the music industry. Those people who gave up at least are no longer in your way, which means there are less people with which to compete. The longer you wait, the shorter the line gets from you to your opportunities.

The people who have the power to give you opportunities are being approached all day everyday for those opportunities. I don't believe that they purposely crush dreams, this industry moves very fast, so, by the time you leave their presence, if you don't find a way to stay on their mind, you are forgotten and they move on to finish that gig and get another one.

The purpose of this entire networking dance is to become a "first call" musician, producer, composer, singer, or whatever it is you want to become. Just like the name says, a "first caller" is the first person that gets thought of whenever a job or gig comes up. You may get quite a few "no's" before you get to the "yes" that will change your career. Think of all of the "no's" as a part of the weeding out process and know that your "yes" is inevitable.

Each "no" brings you one step closer to your "yes". Beginning your journey to become a "first caller" teaches you the critical skills to "make things happen." You begin to use your creativity to make new connections and create gigs for yourself. This process keeps you fresh and on top of your game. It is in this place that you will develop the skills and knowledge to become a professional first call musician. Look at this journey as a rite of passage.

Some people along the way want to see if you can handle the advice they give you, and if you actually will implement their suggestions. Once you have proven yourself, you will be handed the keys to go to the next level. One day, you will be the gatekeeper helping others achieve their dreams. Networking will never end, though; you'll have to be shaking hands for a long time, even when you have reached your original goals.

I FINISHED MY CD, WHAT'S NEXT?

First of all, congratulations on finishing your CD! I'm sure you put sweat and tears into the musical production, you checked out all of the artwork, and you lost hours of your life listening to the same songs over and over again. But what good is a CD, if it's not being heard?

The next step is distribution. In this day and age, digital is the easiest way to distribute your CD. Some people are still buying physical CDs, but those people are in the minority. Now, with smart phones, tablets, Mp3 players, and so on, most people simply just decide to go the completely digital route.

If you are looking for online distribution, there are so many sites available these days, that it can be a bit overwhelming. Most of the sites out there will give you a "free" version of their software, like *Reverbnation™, Nimbit™ and SoundCloud™*. However, if you really want to take advantage of their full exposure, you'll have to spend some money. In most cases, you'll have to spend a little over $300 per year in order to be distributed on sites like *Amazon™, CDbaby™, Itunes™,* and so on.

One that I personally find interesting is *Tunecore™* (*www.tunecore.com*). I had such a great experience with them, and their prices are incredibly reasonable. New sites are popping up everyday, so doing an internet search periodically on the phrase, "online music distribution," will keep you pretty current. Check reviews, and be patient.

Remember that these websites will put your music out there for the world to see, but it will still come down to you doing the work to promote it and generate sales. The only real way to make people realize that you are an artist or band to reckon with is to show them what you do best. You can't simply just rely on chance for things to happen. Action is what moves you forward, and even though you may have gotten this far, you still need to continue to invest more time and energy into your project to "ensure" success.

The market for physical CD sales is becoming more of a "memento purchase," for when you see a band live or when you attend a concert. A lot of musicians are evolving from CDs to recording their music on flash drives. You might say, well where can I get a whole bunch of flash drives for a cheap price? Believe it or not, you can order customized Flash drives from a wide array of websites that will design the drive with your logo and your music embedded already. *Alibaba.com* is one place I found.

***NOTE: Just like physical CDs, flash drives cost to be produced. It is better to get flash drives once you have a decent following and are doing shows on a consistent basis.*

> *That way, you know you have a chance of selling your drives. The cool thing about a flash drive with your logo on it is that it is publicity for you. Whoever sees the flash drive now has heard of you.****

The great thing about being an artist today is that you don't have to pay a lot of money to make your music available for people to buy. For artists with no money at all to spend, I recommend this plan.

1   Go to *wix.com* and create a website. Yes, that's right, it's free to build your own website with your name. *Wix.com* has a lot of cool templates for you to start with, as well. If you have a small budget, you can get a website built by a professional, using one of the outsourcing sites. Whatever you do, you have to have a website. Research other artists to get an idea of what you need.

2   Go to *paypal.com* and open a business account with them. If you have an iPhone™, you can download an app called, "PayPal Here." Once you sign in, PayPal™ will send you a credit card reader that lets you accept credit cards.

With the app, you can also accept checks by taking a photo from your phone. It takes a few days for a check to clear and then it goes directly into your PayPal™ account.

3 Go to *myspace.com*, and create a music account. If you already have one, dust it off. *Myspace.com* is free and is an easy way to have a place to sell your music. You simply upload your music, and set the price.

Once you sell a few CDs, you can then use a site like *tunecore.com* to distribute your album online to sites like iTunes™, Amazon™, etc.

You will have to make a few physical CDs, even though you are doing online distribution. The reason being, you have to be able to send out press kits. Most radio stations, managers, and venues want a physical CD in a press kit. This CD doesn't have to be shrink wrapped like the store would want it. You can burn a few CDs and place your contact information on the cover of the CD and the physical CD itself. If you want your CD to look more professional, you can use *lulu.com* or another print on demand site to print a few CDs at a time. This is also really great if you have a show coming-up, and you want to only get fifty to one hundred CDs printed at a time. We'll get into more detail about PR kits, later.

Finally, you have your site up and your music is available online. Most people assume that once their music is up, they will immediately start making millions, and be able to quit their job; it's not that easy. The final piece is marketing.

Marketing on a budget isn't difficult, you just have to be creative. Instead of always asking people to buy your CD, why not treat them like they are your friends who just so happen to be online? They feel connected to you, and now want to support you in whatever way they can.

Another trend that has been huge in recent years is posting videos on *YouTube™* of you covering popular songs. If people like your video, you can direct them to another website where they can buy your CD. I know I lightly touched the surface of marketing, but don't worry; there is a later section devoted to marketing.

"Be wise and never leave any part of your career solely in the hands of anyone. You, alone, are responsible for your success!"

~Andrae Alexander

BOOK THREE

GETTING YOUR MESSAGE TO THE MASSES

At this point, you should have an idea of the journey some of your favorite artists have taken to be successful. This book is all about taking action; to get the full benefit, you have to take action, and do the steps in every section. I've organized the sections so that each one builds upon the previous section.

After reading this book, you will be able to guide your career in whatever direction you want. Implementing the techniques that follow will help you to stand out as a professional. Take your time and do everything to the best of your ability; doing a rushed job does more harm than good. A few minutes a day working towards your goal is better than taking on more than you can handle and quitting, never finishing.

See you at the end,

Andrae

CREATE YOUR ROAD MAP

It is very important to have a physical "road map," otherwise, you will never know if you are actually going in the right direction or going in circles. There are so many musicians that focus solely on their craft. That is awesome, however if you are the best singer in the world, but no one ever hears you, what is the point?

The truth is that you have to be the best musician you can be, as well as the best marketer, stylist, web designer, and everything else that you can be, as well. If you do not have a clear vision for where you want to go, as well as a way you envision getting there, you will be lost. There are many great songs written that you will never hear, not because of lack of talent, but lack of planning. You need to create a clear path towards your own success, and this is exactly what we will be doing.

Instead of trying to map out the progressive steps from the current situation towards the ideal situation, we are going to work in reverse. The question that you'll need to ask over and over again is the following: "What do I need to do to achieve this?" Starting from the "ideal situation," work backwards. When answering the question you should look at things like:

- Resources needed

- Contacts
- Skills to acquire
- Equipment
- Etc.

When you are done, it will look like a ladder going from your current situation to your ideal situation. For Example:

Compose for seven feature films

Find a student director and score three films for him for free

Compose ten songs in the style of films I like

Learn to read music

Learn to play the piano

Learn the names of the composers who score the types of films I like

Figure out what types of films I would like to score

I like watching films

Once you have created a map that clearly shows you how to get from one step to the next, start to take the steps. Place the list of your steps where you go to create your songs, and cross off each listed step as you finish.

Don't rush the process in a few weeks; know that it may take you a year or more. If you give yourself time to go through the list and diligently work, you will be surprised at how much closer you will be to your goals.

The more detailed steps you have, and the smaller the intervals are between each step, the clearer your road map will be. Don't be afraid to change your steps as you learn. You may start off wanting to score film, but then realize you love playing the guitar on tour; that's okay, go with that, and see where it takes you.

Remember, plan from your ideal situation to your current situation. You should also be aware that every step you advance, more tasks will be included. Even though you have worked on a detailed plan, plans hardly work out perfectly. You need to be flexible, but you should have a road map to measure your success.

This strategy works in almost every aspect of your life, and I strongly suggest that you make it a habit. Those who know where they want to go, and those who have a general idea of how to achieve success, are more likely to enjoy the fruits of their actions. I include in the back of the book a chart entitled "Road Map," this way all you have to do is fill out the boxes and start on the journey of creating you career.

Make a Press Kit

A Press Kit or a Press Release Kit is a promotional tool that tells the world who you are as an artist, what you look like, what you sound like and how much you are in demand. You send them to record labels, festivals, and venues, where you are interested in performing. For this reason, attention to detail is a must.

Most of us wouldn't want a person who is rude, illiterate, has an offensive odor, or wears too small clothes to represent us. The reason is not that we think they are horrible people; they just don't represent us well. Take a few moments to describe yourself as an artist. For this example, I will use the words "energetic," "fun," and "youthful."

Now that we have a description, let's apply that to the different components of the kit. Before we move on, let me list those components.

1. Cover

2. Photo

3. Bio

4. Music

5. Video

6. Press

Let's look at each piece of the kit individually.

COVER

This is the first thing the recipient of the kit sees, the first impression of you. You don't have to spend a lot of money on this, but you should try to put your personality into it. Going back to my description of being energetic, fun, and youthful, I wouldn't go to the store and get a plain manila folder. I may get a neon green folder, and put a sticker of my band logo or name on it. I would also have my contact info here as well.

PHOTO

If a picture is worth a thousand words, make sure you take your time and plan those words carefully. Since we are going for energetic, fun, and youthful, your photo should show that. A photo of you in vibrant colors, and smiling, while performing a concert to a thousand college students who have posters with your name on them, would portray energy, fun, and youth, to me.

Besides putting your creativity into how you're dressed, how your hair and makeup is done (yes, guys, you too should have a makeup artist for a professional shoot), and the location, also take the time to try different angles; some angles make you look better than others.

BIO

When it comes to a bio, my advice is to write it for where you see yourself in five years. Instead of talking about the talent show when you were five, tell us about your musical influences, major gigs that you've done, successful people with whom you've worked, places you've been, and, of course, where you are going as an artist.

Don't be afraid to describe yourself as you see yourself, and be confident. This is where you have the gift to tell people who you are, so, don't miss the opportunity. For example, "energetic, fun, and youthful are words that describe (insert your name here). If Lady Gaga and Pee Wee Herman had a child, it would be (insert your name here)."

MUSIC

Being that this is the music industry, your music has to be the best it possibly can be. Pick your top four to five songs, placing the best one first, and burn it on a CD. Put it in a CD sleeve or CD jewel case. Make sure your contact information is on the CD cover and the actual CD itself. It's okay if you have to burn a CD yourself, as long as you clearly label the CD with your contact information and have great music, you'll be fine.

Just like every other piece in the kit, make sure the music you pick is of great quality and lets the recipient know who you are as an artist. It would be very confusing to get a neon green package with great photos of you crowd surfing, but a CD with you singing all ballads.

VIDEO

If you have decent video footage of you performing, I would suggest you hire a video editor to take the best parts of your performances and put them together as a "demo reel." This shows how you interact with a crowd, and presents your polished show. As a side note, use these videos to analyze your performance and improve; this is one of the best things you could do for yourself as an artist.

PRESS

Every time someone blogs, writes an article in a newspaper, or speaks well about you on camera, you need to try your best to get a copy. Quoting reputable news sources and popular blogs gives you the social proof that will get you better gigs and even a record deal, if you want one.

In your bio, you can use quotes from the press you've received, or be more creative. Making a page that has all of the top quotes, with their sources, could be a great addition to your kit, as long as it drives home the point of you being energetic, fun, and youthful, for example.

Theses are the pieces of a Press Kit, there is also an Electronic Press Kit or EPK. It contains the same information in digital form, and you email it instead. For the EPK, attach your bio and photos to the email, add links to your music (*SoundCloud*™ is great for this), links to your videos (*YouTube*™ or *Vimeo*™ is great for this), and links to your press. There are also sites that are great for helping you put together a great EPK: *Artistecard.com* has a great way to make an EPK, as well as *reverbnation.com*, my favorite because of price and features.

Make sure there is continuity to every piece in your kit; try to make going through your Press kit an experience rather than a formality. Put your name and contact information throughout; this protects you just in case pieces fall out of the kit.

The one mistake that many artists make is to not include their contact information on every piece. You've spent all of this time making sure every piece of your press kit is as good as it can be, you send it to a music festival, but never get a call back. Years later, you realize you never put your name, contact number, and email address for where you can be reached on every item.

Be creative, and make sure this kit represents who you are as an artist. You, as an artist, gets better over time; make sure you are constantly updating your kit to show that. Videos are the easiest and best way to show the energy of your performances and how the crowd receives you.

GET GIGS

Performing is a major part of being an artist; this is where the rubber meets the road. Preparation is key when looking for places to perform. At this point, you should at least have a website, press kit, and great music. Having publicity and great reviews of any kind would be great, as well; if you go in to this process with the same mindset as you have when you're interviewing for a job, you will do great.

Picking a place to perform is where you should start. Asking fellow artists in your area, and doing an internet search will give you a list of the typical spots to perform. Finding spots that are not typical will take some creative thinking, or a simple walk through a few neighborhoods.

There are two types of venues: the venues that everyone goes after, and the venues that no one knows about yet. Of course, I recommend finding venues that aren't over populated with artists; venues like art galleries, casino restaurants, lodges, parks, pavilions, stores, or music studios are places that most artists may overlook.

Once you find a venue, just go in and ask who to talk to about performing. Once you have a name and number, don't be annoying, but be very persistent. If you call and don't get a return call, after two to three days, call back. Always be friendly, most of the time the venue is swamped with calls.

A few things to consider when booking venues are what equipment is available at the venue has, how much walking traffic does the venue gets, and parking. A venue that has instruments and a sound system, is located in an area with ample parking, and is in the center of the happenings in your town is a great venue. Don't ever assume anything when it comes to a gig.

Questions to ask:

1. **Do you provide instruments (piano, drums and bass, and guitar amps)?** If yes, can I come to check them out before my gig? Pianos can be out of tune, and the sound system may only accommodate you and a harmonica.

2. **How do I get paid?** Do you pay me a fee and keep the rest of the money of the door? Do you take 10 percent of the door and keep all of the money you make on the bar and food? Do you pay me a fee, but if we reach a certain number of people give me an increase? There are a lot of scenarios, don't be afraid to ask for what you want.

3. **What is the capacity of the room?** Knowing this lets you know how much money you can potentially make at the gig and how many people to invite.

4. **How do you promote your shows?** Do you take out ads in the paper, or do you just post on your social media sites? This lets you know how much work you will have to do to fill the place.

5. **What time is load in and sound check?** This is very important; you always want to make sure you have enough time to set up and check your sound.

6. **How many comp tickets do I get?** You use these tickets for friends, other venue owners, promoters or bloggers, and media. You would be surprised at how few artists think to give the media free tickets and V.I.P. access to their show.

7. **Can I sell CD'S and Merchandise?** Just so you know, some venues expect a percentage of the sell of your merchandise. If they don't talk about wanting a cut, don't bring it up.

8. **Does the venue provide food for you and your band?** This is always a plus; always ask if it's possible.

9. **Is there a dressing room?** It's always a plus to be able to change and have privacy to get into performance mode.

What most artists realize after they start gigging, but soon find out, is that every aspect of a venue equates to money. The less the venue does, the more you have to do. If there is no equipment, you have to rent it, if they don't comp tickets, you have to pay for the extra tickets. You should always promote your shows even if the venue promotes; you would rather have too many people come than not enough. The more people, the more potential to make money from merchandise and more of an opportunity to get new fans.

CHARGE TO PERFORM

How much to charge is a question that every artist has to answer. To be able to answer this question properly, you have to know what is your end goal and at what stage you are in your career . I can't tell you your end goal, however, I can give you advice on how to progress to the next stage of your career. In this section, I'll go through some ways to put yourself in the position to make more money, before giving you reasonable prices to charge.

Before you can achieve your goal, there are steps that have to be covered. Think about it; if you've never performed before, do you think you should be paid as much as Beyonce'? Artists that are paid the most have a proven track record of successful performances, and a large number of active fans.

To make this clear, I've broken this into "The 3 E's:" Experience, Excellence and Exposure. Though I can't guarantee success, I know that anyone putting this concept into practice is closer to success than failure.

"It may take quite a few tries, but it only takes one time to succeed to be considered a success."

~Andrae Alexander~

Benjamin Franklin was known to say, "Experience is the best teacher, but a fool will learn from no other." The second half of this phrase is what most of us miss. If a fool will learn from no other, it's safe to say that a wise person will learn from others. The fastest way to gain experience is not by doing 1000 gigs, that would take a while.

Finding successful artists and studying them is the best way to gain experience. Study their musical style and what makes people love them. Study their performance style and what about them moves people. Last but not least, study their interview style and what makes people intrigued by them. Do this with a few artists, and you will have a decent grasp of what excellence looks, sounds and acts like.

After you know what this looks like, go out and practice putting that same level of excellence into your music, performances and interaction with your fans. Knowing and performing your artistry at the level of excellence is great, however, if no one notices, who cares. Exposure is the key to commanding the rate that you want.

Exposure is not hard, it just takes time and persistence. At this point in history, social media is the easiest and most inexpensive way to gain exposure to fans all over the world. If you want to get fans in Japan, you can literally go online and add music lovers from Japan to your *Twitter*™ page, and *voila'*, new potential fans in Japan.

Another great way to gain exposure is to have other people talk about you, for example; blogs, newspaper/print, and radio interviews are great ways to gain exposure to potential fans. Although I go into more detail about marketing and promotion in other areas of the book, I can't stress the importance of it enough.

Before I move on, a word of caution. Not devoting focused time and energy on "The 3 E's" will stifle your career, creativity, and potential for success. Just like it took time to learn to sing or play an instrument, "The 3 E's" require time to perfect.

When dealing with how much to charge, you need to calculate how many members there are in the band, whether you have "roadies", if you are the opening act, and so forth. Opening acts charge a lot less; a lot of times, they don't get paid at all to open for acts with a large number of fans. Yes, you need to play for "free". In many cases, your "payment" can be publicity, exposure, video, and so forth. So, measure out what you need, and make the assessment based on that.

What you need to do is:

- Calculate how many band members or staff members there will be

- Assign an amount of money you want to pay to each one. For example, $100 per musician and $50 per Roadie. Then all you need to do is count how many people will be participating and calculate the total.

- Calculate how much you need to spend to get there. (gas, car rental or bus fare)

- Make sure that drinks and food is included in the offer (water, RedBull™, etc.)

- Take that total and add 15 percent more on it. So, if your sum of musicians and staff members came to $500 then you'll charge $575 plus (costs for gas, food and drinks)

Why would you charge 15% more? I am assuming you don't have a manager, and if you do, the 15% goes to the manager. If you don't have a manager, the 15% goes to the band, to print out new PR kits, to pay for gas, and so on. To make sure you are set up to make money for future gigs, get a friend to take photos of you performing, and keep a log of the places you have performed, including the number of people at each venue.

As you get better gigs, venues will want to see you perform and know how many people come to your shows. Having this information on hand will save you time. Once you are able to, by using videos and social media, proving that you can fill a venue, you can start to charge more. Selling CDs, t-shirts, and other merchandise will dramatically reduce the number of gigs you have to do to reach your financial goals.

You might think that having roadies is an additional expense that can be cut, and while this is true, you need to think about the psychology behind having roadies. When an unknown band walks on stage and a couple of staff members (wearing the band shirt and written in big white letters on the back "roadie") you'll achieve a couple of things. The first thing is that you'll appear to be more "pro" than bands that don't have it, and, second, having someone else set up for you will allow you to focus on performing. As your career grows, these elements become almost mandatory because life can get really hectic when you are "gigging."

You know your price will increase the more you play. For the first three paid gigs, let's say you charge $500 USD. When you hit the fourth one, then, you should increase your fee by at least 10 percent to 20 percent. Why? The reason your fees begin to increase periodically is because the value of your band is increasing. When you started out, you had no fans, but, after a couple of gigs, you could have more than 1,000 fans.

You now have more influence, which means that there is a possibility of 1,000 people showing up to your gigs. For a venue, this is gold, since those same 1,000 people will be spending money on drinks and so forth. So, as your fan base grows, remember to adjust your fees. In the end, there is no limit to how much you can charge per venue; the ideal would be to be able to organize your own concerts and make money off of the tickets and goods.

Work on "The 3 E's" and the money will increase periodically. Remember:

Band Members + Staff Members + Expenses = Total + 15% of total = How much to charge.

USE TOOLS ONLINE TO GAIN EXPOSURE

Ever since the dawn of *Myspace*™, musicians have had the ability to share their music in a new and unique way. These days, there are many different types of online music platforms that you can use to promote your music. In this section, I will talk about a few of them, as well as features to look for in future promotional tools.

SoundCloud™

With SoundCloud™, you will have the ability to upload your music, to share it seamlessly with Facebook™, and also sell your music. As is the case with all of these online platforms, you have the option to make a free account with limited options, or you could spend money for the premium memberships. The free membership isn't bad, in fact, it gives you a lot of space with which to work. The difference between free memberships and the premium membership is that the premium memberships typically give you access to more tools that help you learn who are your fans.

I use SoundCloud™ when sending links to potential clients; it has a great feature that allows you to have music posted in a private setting that can only be accessed with a link. It is also a great way to find out about new music, and to share your new music with people who are seeking something different.

Reverbnation™

One of my favorite sites for artists, Reverbnation™, not only has a great platform for you to connect with venues, fans and other potential clientele, the team at Reverbnation™ also works hard to put the artists associated with them in front of music industry professionals. The one thing that Reverbnation™ does better than just about everyone else is find gigs; the street marketing isn't bad either.

As with all the other websites out there, this one also has a free and "premium" membership. Unlike SoundCloud™, this one gives you ample opportunity for distribution. Not only do they have a very cool app for your Facebook™ page, they also distribute on all the major retail websites such as Amazon™ and iTunes™.

The overall price is also a lot cheaper than SoundCloud™, coming to about $300 per year for the biggest upgrade. Reverbnation™ also sends you invites to festivals and other exclusive deals, such as radio promotion; I get at least three to five event invites per month. Their apps that help you sell music through smart phones and tablets aren't too shabby either.

Nimbit™

Not only do they have a great name, the industry giant, Presonus™, brings this platform to you. Nimbit™ mostly caters to Facebook™, if you want to have a Facebook™ store that surpasses all the others, Nimbit™ is the way to go. Again, you have the option of choosing the free and paid memberships. Personally, I would invest in the paid membership because of the Facebook™ marketing capabilities.

Tunecore™

Tunecore™ is how you get your professionally recorded, mixed and mastered music into online stores for distribution on iTunes™, Amazon™, and many more stores in the U.S. and internationally. The reason I chose to feature Tunecore™ is the fact that you pay them yearly, and then you are done.

It would be great if the artists had access to the email contact information of the fans who paid for their music. Unfortunately, the online stores don't provide the artist with that information.

Features to Look Out For:

- Easy to use
- Gives you access to emails

- Allows you to sell your music and merchandise
- Looks great
- Has a large number of music lovers visiting each month
- Gives you creative freedom over your career

Technology changes, but your needs as an artist doing business will be fairly consistent. Before you make a decision to use any service, know what you are trying to accomplish. If you don't have any music recorded yet, is it wise to get a *Tunecore*™ account? Probably not; get your music recorded first. Use the roadmap you created earlier; this will save you a lot of money. This will also help you to stay focused.

GET DISCOVERED... OR NOT!

Today being "discovered" means a lot of different things. You could be discovered by a major record label, a world famous producer, or simply put up a video on YouTube™ to be discovered by the world. From talking to artists, I know this question is usually about being discovered by a major label.

How to get discovered by a major label -- this is harder than it seems, and, in my personal opinion, not the best way to go. If you sell 50,000 copies of your album independently, you have made more money than if you were to sell 1,000,000 records through a major label. You also get to keep all of your rights and royalties. If you are still sold on the idea of "being discovered" by a major label, the following is what you should do.

Make everything associated with you, as an artist, as professional as possible. This means websites, all of your social media, CDs etc. The fact that technology has advanced to the point where a free website can be almost as sophisticated as a $3,000 website is a good and bad thing. You now have to present yourself to the label as a finished product, with fans and all.

They want to see album sells, shows booked, *Twitter*™ numbers, as well as *YouTube*™ video views, that rival their present artists. To stand out, you need to be creative. Be creative with the videos you shoot and promote, as well as with the music you create. You shouldn't try to be Katy Perry; they already have one of those, so, be the best you.

Having a manager who either has connections to major labels or has the tenacity to get you in meetings with major labels, will also help. If, as an artist, you haven't done the work to prepare for a meeting with a label, all of the connections in the world can't help you. Labels pick up artists that are "sales worthy," which means, if they don't think you're going to sell albums, they won't sign you.

Music director, Rickey Minor, once said to me, "When swimmers want to join the Olympics, they go to where the Olympics swimmers swim. Why do musicians think it's different for them?" This is great advice, if I've ever heard any. If you know where musicians or artists who are signed hang out, frequent that spot, and try to get a performance there.

This will allow you to be seen and known by the key players in your area. Send out your PR kits to record labels. Before doing this, there are a few things that you need to research. Blindly sending out materials is a waste of your and the record label's time.

First, make sure that the record labels you are interested in sign artists that do your style of music. Sending your best Hip-Hop records to an Indie-Rock label would be funny, but not productive. If you are unsure of your style, research artists that are similar to you, and figure out what labels they use.

Next, find out how many artists the label currently has on its roster. I recommend going with a label that is small enough to give your project the attention that it needs. There are a lot of great labels with decent budgets that will devote all of their resources on an artist in which they believe; a lot of these smaller record labels even have major label affiliations. Why go for the top five labels that everyone else is seeking, if there are smaller labels that will give you their focus?

Finally, make sure that the labels you have chosen accept unsolicited material. You can find this out by calling and asking. Once you find out that they do, ask them to tell you how they prefer to receive music fro artists, and to whom you should send your press kit.

To be clear, a label doesn't want to spend a whole lot of money or time on "making the product." Labels want to find someone who is already established. Starting out independently by creating and selling your own CD, loading up videos on YouTube™ and getting great numbers on them, making your Facebook™ fan page and getting fans, as well as having a lot of Twitter™ followers, all help your cause. Once you are making money by yourself, the chances of being picked up by a label increases.

While I am on the subject of videos, I can't stress to you enough how important they are to building your career. A rule of thumb that I teach people: leave cheesy home videos to cheesy artists. The content, quality, and frequency of your videos are of extreme importance when gaining views and fans on YouTube™.

Make sure the content represents you as an artist. The quality of your videos should be the best that you can make it, with great audio and quality picture. Don't be afraid to be creative with camera angles. Twitter™, Facebook™, SocialCam™, and whatever new video site that pops up are great, just be current with all social media.

I know I've said it before, but it is easier than ever to create your own path to success as an artist. After doing so much work to impress a major label, you will have already laid a solid foundation to making and keeping money in your pocket. Using sites like *tunecore.com*, you can distribute your own music to iTunes™. Having a great social media fan base gives you access to fans all over the world that will buy your music and come to shows. You are already creative; if you use that same creativity in promoting yourself, you will see great results.

SEND MUSIC TO RECORD EXECUTIVES...OR NOT!

As we discussed in the previous question, having your career in order is the best way to start. Record execs probably receive hundreds of songs from artists everyday, so the trick is to make sure you stand out. Having your photos, videos, social media and music on par with artists signed to major labels is the first step in standing out, here are a few more ways.

Again, know to whom to send your music. You can't expect to send a packet to a record label addressed only to the label, and expect it to end up in the right hands. Go online, or call the label to find out to whom you should address your package. Again, find out if they accept unsolicited material. If they don't, an entertainment attorney will either be able to send the material for you or point you in the direction of someone who can.

Even if you address your package to the specific exec, there still are several hundred other artists that did exactly the same. Therefore, you need to work on your presentation and pitch, as well. Find a unique way of sending your material. You need to paint a picture to the exec about you as an artist, give them samples of your music and video links to watch. Maybe you can even include some tickets to your next show.

I have heard of some people sending their PR kits in a pizza box addressed to the exec. This way, the PR kit is delivered directly to the person of interest, and there is almost no way that it will be overlooked. If you're planning on sending it this way, remember to wrap your PR kit in plastic. Did this actually work? I have no clue. ☺

The point is to be creative, and think of a method that hasn't been used before. Try different forms of communication; regular mail, faxes and even telegrams. Why not? Be creative in your delivery, be professional in your PR kit, and send it out to as many relevant labels as you can. Don't place all of your hopes in one label. The best-case scenario would be to have multiple labels wanting you.

In my opinion, it is better to stay independent than to sign with a label. Certain labels will sign a contract with you and then never release your music. It's called, "being shelved." If you sign, make sure you have a guarantee that you won't be shelved. If you seem like competition to a band that a label wants to promote, then they could come to you with a contract only to shelve you. Hire a reputable music entertainment attorney with a roster of current artists and musicians that he or she represents, don't be afraid to shop around.

Get Your Music on the Radio

Before you begin the process of trying to get your music on the radio, make sure your online presence is professional, and your music is at the highest quality that you can make. Make sure that your music is professionally mixed and mastered. Having a great PK and (EPK) is a great idea, too. These things will give you a better chance at getting air play.

Many commercial radio stations are run by major corporations. These major corporations deal with other major corporations, in this case, the major record labels. As a business this makes since. Commercial radio stations typically make money from companies that pay them to run advertisements or commercials on their stations. The more listeners, the more money they can charge for running ads.

If I were charging for advertisement for my radio station, I would want artists with the most notoriety, marketing, and promotion behind them as I could get. This means that my listeners will have a greater chance of knowing these artists and want to hear them. The more listeners, the more I can charge for advertisement.

A major record label, with a marketing and promotions department, can guarantee that the artists they submit to commercial radio stations will have a decent amount of marketing behind them. That being said, it's hard for an indie to get on most major radio stations because of their lack of marketing.

Hard does not mean impossible. As an indie artist, at this point in music history, you are alive to be a part of a shift in power. This shift has taken the focus from music lovers finding new music by only listening to commercial radio, to music lovers surfing all over the Internet at sites like _unsigned.com_ and _facebook.com_ to find music they love.

This shift in power has caused many labels to downsize and revamp how they promote and market music. This is where you come in; you have the opportunity to create what radio means to you. To all of the traditionalists who want their music to be played on the radio, I offer this advice: focus all of your efforts on listener-supported, non-profit, non-commercial radio stations in your chosen area.

Doing an internet search will help you to find these stations in the area you choose. For example, if I want to find listener-supported radio stations in the Washington, D.C. area, I would type "listener-supported radio station in Washington D.C.". When I did this search, WPFW 89.3 came up, among other stations.

After you have a list of the stations in the area that you choose, make sure that they play the type of music that you perform. If you are a Rock artist, it would not make since to send your music to a Classical station. This would be a waste of time. Once you have a list of stations that are non-commercial and play your style of music, you should now check the stations' programming.

Programming is simply the schedule of when shows air on any particular station. What you are looking for are shows that would best fit your music and the name of the DJ or host. Once you have a list of programs and the name of the host, look for this person's contact info. On most sites, this is not hard to do. If it is not on the site, do a quick internet search.

Another person to get the information for is the program director of the station. The program director has the ultimate say so on what gets played on that radio station. Get his contact info, as well. After your search, you should have names and contact info for DJs, hosts, and program directors for every station in which you are interested.

The next thing to do is contact them, inquiring about the best way to submit your music to be put in rotation. This initial email should introduce you as an artist, as well as have links to where they can hear your music. Keep it short and straight to the point. A short bio with links to your music is good.

From my experience, they usually get back to you saying, yes, we like it, or no, thank you. If you don't get a reply in about two to three days, it's okay to send a follow-up email. Always remain polite, never seem angry or impatient. Persistence, not annoyance, is the goal. After the first and second email are sent, contact them again when you have an event. Don't be surprised if they invite you to be a guest on their show.

A very overlooked radio market is college radio stations. They typically are non-commercial and are willing to play indie artists' music. Satellite radio is another option for getting airplay. The same steps of finding the shows that are best for your music, getting contact information for the DJ, host and program director still apply.

Be ready to send in a physical CD to the station, if you are chosen. This CD should be clearly marked with your name and contact info on the sleeve of the CD, and on the actual CD itself, and the names and order of the songs clearly marked. It does not have to be pretty, a basic white sticker is alright. Also, it's great to have the instrumental of your song on the CD as well. Instrumentals are used for commercials or to play while the DJ or host talks during the show.

There are also sites like _radioairplay.com_ that will get you played on internet radio stations, and get you real fans by playing you with artists that are already established in your genre. _mp3waxx.com_ is a site that can blast your music to thousands of music industry contacts. If they like your music, and you have a budget, they can also guarantee radio play.

There are other ways to get on the radio, if you are creative. Example: start an event focused on helping a cause, get other performers to perform and donate to non-profits. Approach radio stations, blogs and other media about this type of event, and you will most likely have a press presence. Think creatively.

Before I move on, the popularity of internet radio stations is growing. It is much easier to get on an internet-based radio station than any other station, and you typically only have to deal with one person -- the host or DJ. Also, starting your own radio station on the internet is easy and free, in most cases. This will allow you the opportunity to feature your own music, as well as the music of other artists that you love.

MARKET SUCCESSFULLY

This is one of my favorite topics to talk about; as an artist, you need all of the marketing you can get. Without it, no one knows you. To have a successful marketing campaign, you must know that when you say marketing, you really are referring to three different things:

1. Branding
2. Marketing
3. Publicity

What most artists think of as marketing is actually publicity; that's where you are on TV doing commercials and getting radio interviews. In order to get there, you need to focus on your brand to determine to whom you are actually marketing yourself. Once you know that, you can decide which channels and radio stations you should focus on.

Branding is where you choose what adjectives are associated with you as a product, sound, and everything that's associated with you. *Marketing* is when you tell people about your product. P*ublicity* is when other people talk about your product.

To help you get a clearer understanding, I'm going to focus on each topic. While reading this, I want you to answer the following questions:

1. How do I describe my brand?

2. To whom am I marketing?
3. Where do the people I want to market to go to find new artists?

Let's start with Branding.

Branding

This is how you put your stamp on everything that you do. As an artist, you need to have an idea of what it is you are trying to accomplish. If you just want to make millions of dollars as a singer, and that's it, you will likely be chasing a dream for years to come. As a brand, what void are you filling? How will anyone benefit from buying anything from your brand?

To use everyone's favorite person, Oprah helps women to become their best self. She talks about self-improvement, her guests talk about self-improvement, she does movies dealing with self-improvement, she has a magazine that deals with the same. Do you get the picture? When you buy into her brand you know you're going to feel better and gain confidence in your abilities.

Another example would be Beyonce', she is also about empowering women, however, she does it very different from Oprah. Beyonce's brand is very much about women accepting who they are, taking back their power, and being in control. Her shows are over the top, her style of dress is over the top, her music videos are over the top, and she embraces her sexuality.

Once you know who you are and what is your message, think about what things you want to be associated with you as an artist. This is where you can be creative with products you endorse, the use of costumes in your show that can then be sold as merchandise to your fans, CD covers, and even the subject matter for your music.

A good example of this is the band, Slipknot. They always wear Halloween masks when they perform. This, in my opinion, is branding at its best. They create a sound that is unique to them, and reinforce their uniqueness by adding the visual aspect of the Halloween costumes. They have a band identity that is easily recognized.

Marketing

Marketing is where you tell the world who you are as an artist. The good thing about being an artist in this day and age is that there are many avenues for you to tell music lovers about your music. The bad thing about being an artist in this day and age is that there are many avenues to tell music lovers about your music. I hope you thought that was as funny as I did.

A few years ago, having a lot of fans on Myspace™ and a few hundred thousand views on YouTube™ was enough to get you gigs, boost CD sales, and maybe even a possible look from a record label. Now, the fact that so many artists have taken to social media to build their musical empires has desensitized potential fans from marketing tactics that once were effective. To stand out, you have to have an online presence that is just as professional as your major label funded peers; this is not as hard as it sounds.

Now that we know what your brand looks and sounds like, we have to give it a face. In my opinion, your website should be the hub where potential fans, club owners, agents and whomever else wants to know about you, go to find out about you. I've talked to a few friends who disagreed with the point that Facebook™ and YouTube™ are where everyone connects. My argument is simple: at one point, Myspace™ and AOL™ chat rooms were where we connected, now, we are on to other sites.

As an artist, your livelihood depends on being about selling music to fans, getting those fans to come out to shows, and then being able to sell more music to those fans. If you focus all of your effort on sites like iTunes™, you will continue to struggle. Think about it, you put an album on iTunes™ and get as many people as you can to buy the album. The next album you put out, you have to do it all over again. Again, remember that sites, like iTunes™, will not provide you with the email address to those who initially bought

144

your album. For this primary reason, it is better to focus your efforts on getting fans to buy directly from you. Not only would you not have to share 30 percent of your sales, but you would have a growing email list of people who have already purchased your music. Even when the next wave of social media sites pops up, you still are in contact with your fans.

Saying that, you should still have a Facebook™ fan page, Twitter™, Instagram™, and whatever other social media site that pops up. To keep up with them, there are great sites like Ping™ that will connect all of them for you, leaving you with only having to go to one page to access all of your social media. Use them all, be social and interact with everyone, just remember to get email addresses whenever possible, to be able to connect with them on your owns terms.

YouTube™ is also a great way to market yourself. The best advice I can give you for this is simple: do everything at the best quality you can. Use the best quality camera you can, use natural sunlight whenever possible, or use a light kit to remove shadows, and always use a lapel microphone when doing anything live. This is to eliminate as much noise or ambient sound as possible from your recordings.

So far, I've focused mostly on online marketing: T-shirts, hats, cups, magnets, belts, and anything else you can think of to put your brand on is also great. P.O.D. (Pay On Demand) sites are great, because you don't have to buy anything; your fans buy your products, and another company creates it and sends it to them. Theprintful.com and *teespring.com* are great places to start.

Newspapers typically have an events section. Find out how to get in that section by contacting the writer, or calling the newspaper directly to ask. You can also put an ad in the paper, depending on the popularity of the newspaper; this may not be as expensive as you would think.

Radio ads are always great, and add a level of professionalism to your brand. You can either pay for a DJ to read your ad, or actually record an ad yourself. If the DJ is popular in your area, let him read it; people will assume he's a fan, and come to the show.

Posters and flyers can be great for marketing, if you pay attention to the laws in your area. To make them useful, hire a great graphic designer that will create something that is very eye catching, and clearly tells the viewer what you want them to do.

My final note is, when marketing yourself, always stay true to your brand. If you are known as a kid friendly artist who is very patriotic, don't endorse products that are known to use child workers in China; you may, at the very least, confuse you fans, and at the worst, you may lose your fans. Think through everything that is associated with your brand, before revealing it to the public. Being protective of your image will never hurt you.

Publicity

Speaking of the public, publicity is what gives you the social proof to make people pay attention to you as an artist. This is where others talk about you. My advice, before trying to get more publicity, is to make sure you are confident with your brand, and you have a very professional marketing campaign going. This makes it easier for bloggers and reporters to find information about you. The best part about this is, you told them what you wanted them to know.

Instead of leaving your image to chance, you hopefully took the time to think it through. This doesn't mean that you control everything that is written about you, this does give you a better chance than most, though.

The best way to get publicity is to do something that is newsworthy. Newsworthy is usually something that affects a large number of people, is innovative, or pertains to something that is already "newsworthy". The easiest place to start is to go with something that is already "newsworthy".

For example, if Veterans Day is coming up, you could have a show thanking veterans for their service, and invite Veterans' posts. Now you have people and a holiday that reporters will need to find stories about. Being creative and thinking ahead are the name of the game.

A benefit of getting write-ups is that you are put in front of people who can potentially become fans of yours. Once you get enough publicity, you can go for bigger media outlets, and even TV shows. At first, it may seem difficult to contact bloggers and reporters. Once you get a few responses, you will see that they are just people trying to do a job.

Your job is to make their job easier by thinking ahead for relevant holidays. Even finding blogs that are relevant to you will help you and the blogger out. An example: if you are an artist that happens to wear glasses, why not contact a blogger that writes about glasses? While most artists are going after music blogs, you can build your media presence by going after blogs that other artists over look; take the road less traveled.

MAKE A TOUR

Touring is where musicians really get to make money, if it is done correctly. Don't expect your first tours to be big, or even yours for that matter. There are many ways to tour, and you have to decide, based on your current situation, what direction you should take.

Opening Act

Whenever you go to see your favorite band, there is typically another act or two that performs to warm-up the crowd; those acts are the opening act. If you have been performing and have perfected a great show, but don't have the fan base to do your own tour, connect with local bands who tour, and ask to be their opening act. The opening act may or may not get paid, although you can sell CDs and other merchandise.

Your Own Tour

This is the dream of most artists, to have enough fans to go on a tour. Having had the privilege to go on a couple of tours, let me tell you they are a lot of fun and work. The benefit of touring is that you can get to meet your fans, get more fans, and sell merchandise. At this point, you know how to put on a show and sell merchandise, so, let's get to what else you need to know.

1. **Where are your fans?** Once you know the areas of your fans, make a list of venues in those areas. If you've been tracking album sales, this shouldn't be a problem. If you are unsure, you can just ask your fans.

2. **Start booking the venues.** Try not to book more than one venue in the same city. If you book two venues, you have less of a chance of selling out a show. A sold out show looks great on your musical resume'; this also makes other venues more likely to book you.

3. **How will you travel?** Look at the number of people traveling with you, as well as your budget. Can you afford to rent a tour bus, or will you have to borrow a van? Depending on the length of your tour, buying a decent van may be more cost effective than renting.

4. **Where will you sleep?** Are you going to book hotels every night or at certain points in the tour? Will you all be sleeping in the van? How will you shower? When will you wash clothes?

5. **Who is driving?** Are you paying a driver? Are you and your band taking turns driving?

6. **Make a budget.** Everything you can possibly think of needs to be budgeted. How much money do you need for gas, food, lodging, merchandise, if you sell out, or equipment rental, if something breaks?

I hope you see that with planning and persistence, touring is not impossible. The key to a successful tour is to get enough rest and to plan off days. Don't be overzealous and go a month straight singing everyday. It's hard to keep a tour going when the lead singer has no voice, try to avoid that.

Make Contracts

Hire a lawyer! Hire a lawyer! Hire a lawyer! This is the best advice I can give on creating contracts. I know there are a lot of websites selling pre-made contracts; this has the potential to save you money. If you were to use one of those contracts, not knowing what you are requesting and what you are required to do in the contract, you could potentially lose a lot more money on legal fees.

If you want to save money, find an entertainment lawyer. You wouldn't use a dentist to perform open-heart surgery, so you shouldn't use a lawyer whose focus is on real estate law to negotiate your record deal. Don't be afraid to find a few lawyers and check their client list; a great lawyer will have record labels, as well as artists named.

Do yourself a favor and don't cut corners in this area; asking artists in your circle for help in finding a lawyer is a great place to start. Having a recommendation from a current client is a good introduction, and you will also have a first hand account of your potential lawyers work ethic.

If you really want to know how to deal with contracts, taking a few courses at a community college is a great idea. Now-a-days, you could probably find a course at _coursera.org_, or a host of other sites that offer MOOCs (Massive Open Online Courses). Take advantage of these free opportunities to learn. What you learn today could save you from being taken advantage of tomorrow.

"In today's society, exposure makes you a star in most people's eyes. In my opinion, focusing on exposure alone makes you a shooting star, here today and gone tomorrow."

~Andrae Alexander

CONCLUSION

This book was designed to give you a general "road map" to success as a music artist. Make your map, and start your steps, but don't be afraid to change as technology changes, or as you grow as an artist. As you grow, make sure everything that represents you changes to reflect that growth. When you see artists starting out, give them the help you wish you had when you started.

I think that by sharing knowledge, we obtain new knowledge, so, whenever you find someone in need of guidance or advice, please feel free to pass along wisdom. In the end, it will only benefit you. You never know when someone else will come along and give you that vital nugget of information that you have were needing to reach the next stage in your career.

Remember to treat people with respect, and to continue on your mission, despite what anyone else says. Only you control your happiness. If you deny yourself your own dreams, then you will end up always asking "what if." It takes guts to make it in this industry, and I am sure that if you are reading this book you at least have a seed of what it takes; everything starts as a seed.

Becoming a successful artist isn't the easiest thing on the planet. A lot of times, you'll find yourself wondering if you are actually doing the right thing, or if you are simply wasting your time. The fact is that only you know if you are doing the right thing. Do your music to the best of your ability, giving it all the energy you can. Trying hard and failing gives you great stories to tell; never trying gives you regrets.

I really do wish you great success, and I hope that the information contained in these pages has helped you in achieving your goals. If any of these principles helped you out, why not shoot me an email or post something on my Facebook™ wall; your posts will help motivate your fellow musicians on their paths to success, as well. I also do private consultations, public speaking and music production. If you are interested in using my services, contact me at <u>andraealexander.com</u>.

Don't lose sight of why you became a performer. Don't lose your love and passion for music, and don't forget that music changes situations. Don't take that lightly! Figure out whom you are talking to with your music and how you are helping them, this other stuff is to make sure your fans are able to find you.

RESOURCE SECTION

As promised, in this final section, I will provide you with the tools necessary to achieve your goals. These tools will include checklists, samples, and pretty much everything you need in order to make your life easier. In order to give you the absolute best odds, I have gone to the trouble of creating these elements as samples, which are meant for you to modify to fit your needs. You can take this section as my personal thank you for purchasing this book, a token of gratitude. Good luck!

Resource Checklist

In this section, list everything you have at your disposal; this includes gear, contacts, etc.

Resource Checklist				
No.	Item	Purpose	Availability	Notes
1				
2				
3				
4				
5				
6				
7				
8				
9				
10				
11				
12				
13				
14				

15				
16				
17				
18				
19				
20				
21				
22				
23				
24				
25				
26				
27				
28				
29				
30				

ROAD MAP

Start by filling out the Ideal Situation first, and work backwards until you have reached the Current Situation by answering the question "To achieve 'X' I must first do 'Y'."

1. Ideal Situation

2. Previous step

3. Previous step

4. Previous step

5. Previous step

6. Previous step

7. Previous step

8. Previous step

9. Previous step

10. Previous step

11. Previous step

12. Previous step

13. Previous step

14. Previous step

15. Previous step

16. Previous step

17. Previous step

18. Previous step

19. Previous step

20. Current Situation

You can make this list as long as you need, having twenty steps to begin with is more than enough to get you started and keep you busy for a little while. You can always add more.

Address Book

No.	Name	Profession	Phone No.	Email	Notes
1					
2					
3					
4					
5					
6					
7					
8					
9					
10					
11					
12					
13					
14					
15					
16					

17				
18				
19				
20				
21				
22				
23				
24				
25				
26				
27				
28				
29				
30				

ANDRAE ALEXANDER

INVOICE

Download more invoices for free from
invoicetemplates.org/free-musician-invoice-template.htm

Name of Business (BAND)	
Address:	
Postal Code:	
Telephone:	
E-Mail:	
Invoice to:	
Name:	
Name of Company:	
Address:	
City/Postal Code:	
Telephone:	
E-Mail:	

Description	Amount
Total	$

Press Release Check List

	PR Checklist	
NO	Task	Done
1	Cover Letter	
2	Cover Page	
3	Band Bio or Artist bio	
4	Artist photos or Band Photos	
5	Music Equipment page (Rider)	
6	Booking page/contact info	
7	Demo CD	
8	Song list/Gig sheet	
9	Lyrics Sheet (Optional)	
10	Newspaper Clippings	

| 11 | Band Business card | |
| 12 | Envelope | |

ABC Time Management

A – Urgent and Important

B – Important but not Urgent

C- Not important or Urgent

GEAR GIG LOGISTICS

Item	Amount	Check in	Check out

Signatures			

	IN		
	OUT		

TECHNICAL RIDER

NO.	Item	Who
1		
2		
3		
4		
5		
6		
7		
8		
9		
10		
11		
12		
13		
14		
15		

16		
17		
18		
19		
20		
21		
22		
23		
24		
25		
26		
27		
28		
29		
30		

Made in the USA
Lexington, KY
15 April 2015